CLASSIC ROCK CLIMBS

IN

Northern England

BY BILL BIRKETT

The Oxford Illustrated Press

ACKNOWLEDGEMENTS

Many people have helped in the preparation of this book. I would particularly like to thank the following:

Martin Bagness, Jane Billingham, Dave Birkett, Andy Birtwistle, Andy Blaylock, Chris Bonington, Roger Brookes, Joe Brown, Chris Brueton, John Chettleborough, Sinead Conlon, John Clayton, Ian Dunn, Andrew Earl, John Earl, Dennis Gray, Tony Greenbank, Alison Hargreaves, Trevor Jones, Ian Kyle, Graeme Livingstone, John Lockley, Susan Lund, Colin Matthews, Geoff Milburn, Fiona Mirlees, Majorie Mortimer, Mike Mortimer, Andy Moss, Ian Parsons, Allan Peel, Martin Scrowson, Bob Smith, Fred Snallam, Luke Steer, John White, Iain Williamson.

For correcting the manuscript I would like to thank Susan Lund.

Thanks are due to Martin Bagness for the artwork.

Thanks are due to Paul Renouf of Photo-Scope for black and white printing.

© 1990, Bill Birkett
ISBN 1 85509 208 5

Published by:
The Oxford Illustrated Press Limited, Haynes Publishing Group, Sparkford, Nr Yeovil, Somerset BA22 7JJ, England.

Haynes Publications Inc, 861 Lawrence Drive, Newbury Park, California 91320, USA.

Printed in England by:
J. H. Haynes & Co Limited, Sparkford, Nr Yeovil, Somerset.

British Library Cataloguing in Publication Data:
Birkett, Bill
  Classic climbs in Northern England.
  1. Northern England
  I. Title
  796.522309427
  ISBN 1-85509-208-5

Library of Congress Catalog Card Number:
90-80385

Author's Note
Please note that the climbs in Cumbria are dealt with in *Classic Rock Climbs in The Lake District* by Bill Birkett, published by The Oxford Illustrated Press.

AREA 1: LANCASHIRE

AREA 2: THE PEAK DISTRICT

AREA 3: YORKSHIRE

AREA 4: NORTH YORK MOORS

AREA 5: CUMBRIA

AREA 6: NORTHUMBERLAND

APPENDICES

INTRODUCTION

Following *Classic Rock Climbs In Great Britain* this is the second in a series of individual books to cover the five main climbing areas of Britain. The philosophy behind the series is one of portraying the character of the area and the spirit of some of its most outstanding rock climbs. Whatever the degree of difficulty of the routes chosen, their pedigree or antiquity, they have been selected to display a quality best described as classic.

The rock climbing in Northern England (excluding the Lake District which forms the first book of this series) falls into six independent regions which have been classified thus: Lancashire, The Peak District, Yorkshire, North York Moors, Cumbria and Northumberland. From these areas 57 climbs have been selected. The format of the book is such that there is a fact sheet for each route followed by a summary and description with an accompanying photographic essay of the climb.

Whilst we all climb principally for the fun of it the sport of rock climbing is multi faceted. Firstly there is the pure challenge of rock climbing, the satisfaction of each individual move when strong fingers, good balance and mental control conquer naked rock; on those days the climbing hunger seems insatiable. Secondly there is the wonder of our precious natural environment—many of the climbs here are situated in National Parks designated for their outstanding natural beauty. The areas selected are ideal for the city dweller to easily make the transition from bricks and mortar to the freedom of the wide open spaces; it is only a short journey from the ordinary to a spectrum of experience heightened by your involvement with the rock. Thirdly there is the pleasure of good company; the shared appreciation, knowledge and laughter and the inextinguishable memory of a day well spent. Many sensations, many routes. For these reasons and more it is intended that the classic climbs detailed here will enhance your climbing enjoyment and liberate the free climbing spirit.

The areas are quite distinct in character and history and whilst modern transport means that most people will be able to sample the particular delights of each, their independence and diversity will be found to be one of the most striking attractions of climbing in Northern England. In addition to an overall map of Northern England each area has been sketched to give a clear representation to best show the juxtaposition of the crags.

A fact sheet and route summary provide all you need to locate and follow the line of the route. The summary follows the conventional system of guidebook route description and is taken from first-hand experience. With the advent of modern equipment and rope techniques (see *Modern Rock and Ice Climbing* by the author) the routes described here are primarily single pitch (I recommend 50m length ropes although in most cases 45m would be adequate). Consequently I have described the climbs to accommodate this now usual style of climbing.

The description of the climb constitutes an essay relating not only the facts, the physical moves, possible protection placements, the history, my own adventures, but strives to capture the unique feeling and spirit of the individual route. I have simply written from the heart and my own enjoyment of the climb. I have refrained from describing everything on any particular climb, my intention being to whet the appetite only. The full experience—and many surprises—will only be enjoyed by climbing the routes yourself.

The photographic appreciation of the climbs in colour and black and white is intended to display the particular character of the route and the environment in which it is placed. An overlaid black and white photograph also exactly depicts the actual line of each climb providing a rapid but accurate reference to its location and direction. Achieving high technical standards, being at the right place at the right split second, is not an automatic procedure in rock climbing photography and there have been times when the casual observer may have felt that the photographer was more precariously placed than the subject itself. However, although the plates are intended to accurately record the pure physical involvement, climber to rock, technical perfection is by no means all and I have also taken them to portray something of the climbing spirit; to speak of the excitement, joy, solace, drama, peace and beauty of the wild places and of my great love for climbing.

Route Selection and Difficulty

Although I have climbed all the routes in this book, and a few more besides, it may be thought that I mainly climb in the hard route bracket. This impression would not be wholly correct and I have, since commencing the sport under the guidance of my father, Jim Birkett, appreciated the whole spectrum of climbing experience. For a while now, possibly due to the rather artificial influence of climbing magazines, there has been a tendency for polarisation, with certain groups of climbers missing out on the complete climbing experience. I think my attitude was summed up by Joe Brown, one of the greatest rock climbers, when he said in an interview with Jim Curran:

'I think the important thing about climbing is not what standard you climb at, it's always what you get out of it. I just get so much out of it and, I don't know whether, because my memory is never crystal sharp on some things, or whether it's getting older that makes me really appreciate climbing without taking into account its standard. I have been doing classic climbs for a long time.'

A book such as this must be finite and there are a number of outstanding climbs that could not be included—I apologise. Of course *Classic Rock Climbs in Great Britain* selected nine routes from Northern England and this explains their absence here.

Area Notes

The six different areas warrant some separate introduction and first time visitors to the area may find some interest in the following notes.

Area 1: Lancashire

The climbing here is situated mainly in quarries often sited near the centres of population. Only two locations have been selected and these show a remarkable contrast. Anglezarke is a quarry, but airy and open, situated pleasantly in the moors above attractive reservoirs. The climbing is on a

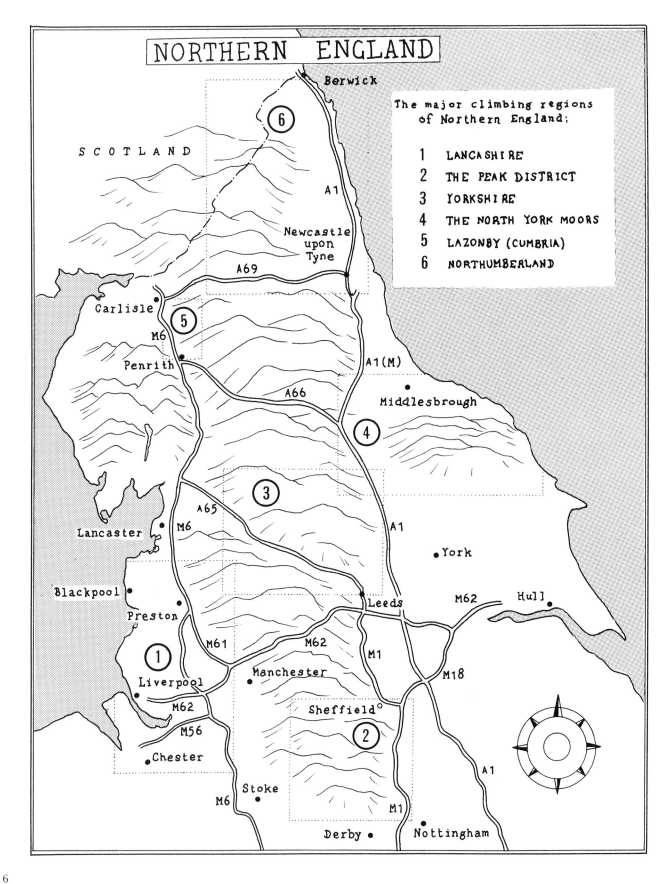

NORTHERN ENGLAND

The major climbing regions of Northern England;

1 LANCASHIRE
2 THE PEAK DISTRICT
3 YORKSHIRE
4 THE NORTH YORK MOORS
5 LAZONBY (CUMBRIA)
6 NORTHUMBERLAND

soft gritstone. The quarry provides perfect evening climbing for those based in Bolton or Manchester and is easily accessible from the M61 passing close underneath. Helsby (geographically in Cheshire), one of the traditional climbing grounds with a history commencing in the 1920s, commands an elevated position above attractive woods looking across the flat plains (now much industrialised) below. It is is composed of red sandstone and easily accessible; the M56 lies directly below, from Liverpool, Manchester and Chester.

Area 2: The Peak District
Probably the busiest pure rock climbing area in Britain. Only a short distance from the major centres of Sheffield, Manchester and Leeds, the Peak is unparalleled in the concentration of routes it has to offer. A National Park, contrasting and intermingling great natural beauty with a rich industrial heritage, it consists of upland moors ringed by gritstone edges and hidden limestone dales. With the immense range of climbing interest from Stanage Edge, the longest grit edge in England, to the magnificent white limestone face of High Tor, it has often been the forcing ground for new standards in technical difficulty. Additionally peak climbing has a long history, that stretches from before the turn of the century, and cut the teeth of such great climbing legends as Joe Brown and Don Whillans. Après climbing in the central Peak inevitably includes Lover's Leap Café (Stoney Caff) and The Moon at Stoney Middleton and Grindleford Station Café (famed for its chip butties).

Area 3: Yorkshire
Rugged grit and delectable limestone back up any Yorkshire climber's claim that his/ her county is the mecca for free rock climbing. Such is the intensity that for some the individual moves on the gritstone of Almscliff or Caley Crags are an end in themselves—the pinnacle of technical rock climbing achievement. So be it and undeniably Malham Cove and Gordale Scar are Britain's most spectacular showpieces of limestone architecture. From the selection of chosen routes great climbing names abound—Arthur Dolphin, Allan Austin, Pete Livesey and Ron Fawcett—all tremendous pioneers who have left an indelible stamp on the climbing world and whose route will leave their own particular mark on you. In this 'chippie and chinkie' kingdom, noted cafés include Pete Livesey's

and Beck Hall (which does incomparably wonderful afternoon teas) in Malham, and Tommy's Café in Ottley. Good pubs abound.

Area 4: North York Moors
Above the chemical and industrial complexes of Teesside rises an area of surprising quality. Moors, hills, valleys and woods that justify its grading as one of Britain's outstanding National Parks. To be found hidden in the hills and folds are many crags of sandstone and a curious rock occasionally rumoured to be limestone. The two crags selected, of the latter type of rock, are worth a visit not only from nearby Middlesbrough but from further afield.

Area 5: Cumbria
Most will associate this newly structured county with the Lake District and rightly so. Yet outside the National Park boundary the Eden Valley offers sandstone climbing of significant importance. Although Carlisle is the nearest centre, many Lakeland-based climbers make this area their second home on rainy or wintery days when sunshine and shelter can often be found here outside the mountains.

Area 6: Northumberland
A forgotten and quiet county, of rolling heathered hills and flat arable plains, situated between the end of the Pennine Chain and the North Sea, England and Scotland. A purple patchwork land alternately wild and cultivated but one which always retains the sweet air of rural independence. The sandstone found here is the firmest in England and indeed is one of the best of all climbing rocks. Excellent friction but not quite so rough as the more southern gritstone. Beneath the austere line of Hadrian's Wall there is another rock to be found— Whin Sill—a unique type of quartz dolerite. Some of the sheltered crags described here are equidistant from the cities of Newcastle or Edinburgh, and as such are uniquely positioned to provide all year round activity. There are many superb routes and good days ahead for those who do not yet know Northumberland. The nearest place to approach anything like a climbing centre is the little town of Belford where there are a number of pubs and a 'chippie '.

Using This Book
Rarely do any of the routes in this book exceed 100ft (30m) in length or attain an

altitude placing them in a mountain context (although some do). This should be carefully noted and it should be understood that the routes are described accepting this. There is no comparison with the climbing here and that on the high mountain crags of the Lake District, Wales or Scotland. That is not to say the climbing is in any way inferior—it is just different. *Vive la différence.*

Within each of the six areas it would be confusing to appoint any specified geographical order and therefore the crags are listed alphabetically. Likewise when more than one climb is described on an individual cliff or edge then the first climb described is generally that nearest the approach path. However in all cases, the position of the route is clearly described and illustrated with the line of the climb marked on a photograph.

For each climb there is an introductory list of information which is mainly self-explanatory but the following comments should be noted.

Access and the Environment: Because a climb is described within this book it does not necessarily mean there is a legal right of access—in many cases there is not. However climbers have long enjoyed a traditional freedom to climb. Often access has only been granted after painstaking negotiations by the British Mountaineering Council or by the local climbing club. To maintain this happy state, strictly observe any restrictions outlined, and respect the crag environment. Do not cause any damage, shut all gates, light no fires and take all litter home (others as well as your own). Look after the crag, the flora and the fauna to preserve this precious world intact for the next generation of climbers. Climbing is largely about freedom therefore do nothing that may give others the right to attempt to curtail it.

First Ascents: This information is given as completely as· is known, but should anyone have any further knowledge then I would greatly appreciate you letting me know.

Grading of climbs: The dual subjective and numerical/alphabetical British system of grading rock climbs has been adopted. The grades apportioned are my own and may be at slight variance with information elsewhere, but should prove consistent throughout the different areas.

Generally within the text only climbs of Hard Severe stature and above have been given a technical grading, e. g. Maloja—45ft (14m), Hard Severe (Overall Grade) (4a)

(Technical Grade of the hardest pitch).

Below is a table showing the Overall Grade, which is an impression grade based on the length and seriousness (difficulty in placing protection) and the range of technical difficulty that may be reasonably expected in this overall grade.

The following is a table comparing the British system of technical grading with some of the most popular grading systems used elsewhere in the world. The table utilises my experiences and those of many others. However, this is not an absolute guarantee of accuracy and is intended as a guide only.

Attitude and Altitude: This information is simple but extremely important if you are to get the best out of the Northern weather. By giving sensible thought to the height of the climb above sea level and the direction in which the climb faces, combined with the seasonal climatical divisions in Britain, routes may be selected that can be climbed throughout all twelve months of the year.

Obviously a south-facing climb will get the sunshine throughout the year: one facing east will get it in the morning; one facing west in the evening and one facing north may never see it at all (depending on the time of the year) or receive its warmth.

The higher the cliff above sea level the colder the air temperature.

Descriptions and Descents: All information (UNLESS stated to the contrary) is given looking at the climb (or crag). Therefore *right* and *left* are relative to the climber *facing in*. This is true for both the climbing descriptions and the descents—because it is usual to work out your descent route from the ground, prior to climbing.

Beware also of rock falls, etc., that may subsequently change the character of the route from that described here.

Dangers: Despite modern protection, or what anyone may say to the contrary, rock climbing is potentially dangerous. Anything less than total concentration, and awareness of the dangers throughout the climbing day can lead to tragedy.

This book assumes a thorough understanding of, and sound practical ability with, all techniques and equipment currently in use in British rock climbing. Beware of rapidly changing weather, particularly in the remoter areas. Always carry adequate clothing, a warm summer's day can rapidly deteriorate.

Photography: All the photography is my own. It is 35mm and is reproduced from colour transparencies and black and white negatives. A variety of lenses have been employed from a wide-angle 28mm lens to a long focal length of 150mm. Further essential information on hill and climbing photography is extensively detailed in the *Hill Walkers Manual* by the author and published by Oxford Illustrated Press.

Good climbing—see you on the crags.

Used Together	
British Overall Grade	British Technical Grade
Moderate	1a
Difficult	2a
Very Difficult	2b
Severe (Mild)	2c, 3a
Severe	3a, 3b
Severe (Hard)	3b, 3c
Very Severe (Mild)	4a, 4b
Very Severe	4b, 4c
Very Severe (Hard)	4c, 5a
Extremely severe E1	5a, 5b
E2	5b, 5c
E3	5c, 6a
E4	6a, 6b
E5	6a, 6b
E6	6b, 6c
E7	6c, 7a

British Overall Grade and Corresponding Technical (Pitch) Grading

Table Comparing International Grading Systems

Britain	France	UIAA	USA	Australia
4a	4 + V	V	5,6	15
4b	5–	V +	5,7	16
4c	5	VI–	5,8	17
5a	5 +	VI	5,9	18
5b	6a	VI +	5,10a	19
		VII–	5,10b	20
5c	6b	VI¹	5,10c	21
			5.10d	
		VII +	5,11a	22
6a	6c	VIII–	5,11b	23
		VIII	5,11c	24
6b	7a	VIII +	5,11d	25
6c	7b	IX	5,12a	26
				27
		IX	5,12b	28
7a	7c		5,12c	
		IX +	5,12d	
	8a	X–	5,13a	

LANCASHIRE—ANGLEZARKE QUARRY

ANGLEZARKE QUARRY: The Golden Tower.
Map Ref: SD 621162.
Guidebooks: *Rock Climbing in Northern England* by Birkett & White. *Rock Climbs in Lancashire and the North West*, Les Ainsworth.
Attitude: Faces west.
Altitude: 600ft (180m).
Rock: Gritstone.
Access: This a sunken and sheltered quarry situated on the edge of Anglezarke Moor. It is only a short distance from the M61. Turn off the motorway at junction 6 and follow the A6027 to the A673 Bolton to Horwich road. Follow left along this and through Horwich to turn right by the Millstone Inn. Continue towards the motorway bridge but turn right just before it is reached. This leads to the Yew Tree Inn. Take the right fork here and continue to cross between the reservoirs. Shortly after this, branch left to follow a steep concrete track into a large car park and picnic area. From the far end of this a path leads out across the road and into the quarry. The Golden Tower is opposite on the far side of the quarry (3 minutes).
Observations: Approaching or leaving Manchester this is a quickly accessible crag suitable as an all year round venue. The sunken quarry is sheltered and has a predominantly friendly nature. Although the rock is generally good it is actually quite soft gritstone and caution should be exercised.

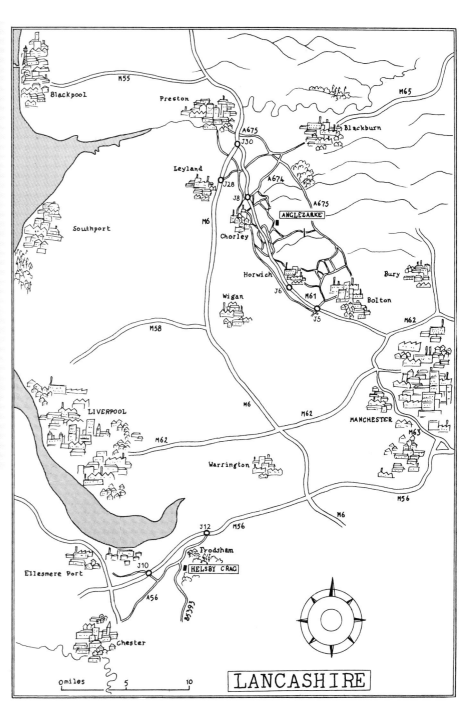

ANGLEZARKE QUARRY: The Golden Tower

THE GOLDEN TOWER: 80ft (24m), E2 (5c).
First Ascent: Les Ainsworth, Ian Cowell (1968).
Location: Golden Tower, Anglezarke Quarry, Lancashire.

The Golden Tower (Summary)

The square cut prow on the far side of the quarry is a prominent landmark. Start from a recess on the left hand side of the front face.

1. 40ft (12m), (5a). Climb the crack to move out right and gain a ledge in the centre of the face. Several belay anchors advised.

2. 40ft (12m), (5c). Climb directly up the wall utilising both the crack and the wall on its right until the shallow groove can be gained and followed to the top.

Golden Tower (Description)

Industrialised Lancashire is a big hearted county which despite its grime and lack of natural rock has produced a prolific stream of rock climbers. Some, such as Joe Brown and the late Don Whillans have become household names. Just why this should be isn't really hard to understand. Rock climbing provides a freedom and perfect release from the industrial grind.

Weekends may see the resident climbing population heading for Wales, The Peak or the Lake District but midweek climbing, in the pre-purpose-built climbing wall era, presented a problem. The solution was the intense development of the man-made quarries. This type of climbing, generally vertical, most often highly technical, and often on rock that could only described as suspect, produces climbers of the highest calibre. From this scenario there are many desperate contenders for the title of the 'last great problem', although outside their locality few would be deemed as great or even a good climb. The exception which stands head and shoulders above its nearest contenders is The Golden Tower of Anglezarke Quarry.

Let's not pretend that it isn't a hard route. It is both very strenuous and technical. But in addition to the sheer challenge that this clean-cut pillar offers the climber it also holds an aesthetic beauty rare in the

O belay point

The Golden Tower

quarry environment. The name says it all, and although it may not be the most practical time to be there, as the sun drops low in the west, The Golden Tower really is golden.

From the ground the steep nature of the rock is immediately apparent. A strong gymnastic attack must be launched. Good jams and a few rickety holds lead to more balancey climbing rightwards over seemingly awkward ledges to the foot of the thin crack. I have described it here as two pitches which may seem unnecessary in the modern world of two ropes and sophisticated runners. Treat it how you wish, but the half-way ledge is not only a convenient place to stop, it marks the division between two contrasting sections of climbing.

This is where the real fun begins and it doesn't seem to matter quite what you do to start. Whether you tackle the crack super-directly or utilise the small holds on the right wall, it has an awkward feel. Any hanging about here is strength sapping and a faint heart will see you reversing back down to the ledge for inspiration. Better to press on if you can.

Success isn't just a matter of brute strength and stamina. Although this is a minimum requirement, there are some specific technical moves here which have to be tackled with thought and precision. Leaving the crack to enter the final vague corner groove is just such a move. Once gained, taking care with the blocks, there is not much of great technical difficulty to reach the top but, countering this, neither is there anything substantial in the way of reassuring protection.

This is something further to think on as you make the typical quarry finish: one where the top is horizontal but otherwise holdless. The hands reach it but you are still on the plumb vertical below. The problem is how do you pull up on a holdless slab? You can't. The solution is to push. So brush away the loose grit particles with one hand, cling on with the other, and then bravely reverse the palms and mantle.

Facing page left: **The Golden Tower.**

Right: **Al Phizacklea jamming up the initial crack of The Golden Tower, with the tower glowing gold in the evening light.**

LANCASHIRE—HELSBY

HELSBY: Flake Crack, Grooved Slab.
Map Ref: SJ 518750.
Guidebooks: *Rock Climbing In Northern England* by Birkett & White.
Attitude: Faces west.
Altitude: 400ft (122m).
Rock: Soft red sandstone.
Access: This crag is situated in a commanding position above the Cheshire Plain. Located on the hillside directly behind the village of Helsby, it is a prominent feature when viewed from the M56. From the village a windy road leads below the end of the crags. Where the road quits the houses and joins the wood there is limited parking on the verge. From here a sandy path leads steeply up to the right end of the crag (5 minutes).
Observations: Although the crag falls naturally into the Lancashire section of this book it is actually located in Cheshire. It is composed of soft red sandstone, good on the routes selected but rather suspect and covered in deep green lichen elsewhere. The crag used to be extremely popular but is now less so. This is a pity for there are some routes here of excellent character and which remain green-growth free.

O belay point

Climbers on Flake Crack.

HELSBY: Flake Crack, Grooved Slab

FLAKE CRACK: 40ft (12m), Very Severe (5a).
First Ascent: Wayfarers' Club (probably
Colin Kirkus), (*circa* 1928).
GROOVED SLAB: 35ft (11m), Hard Severe
(4a).
First Ascent: Wayfarers' Club, (*circa* 1928).
Location: West Buttress, Helsby, above M56
south of Warrington, Cheshire.

Flake Crack (Summary)

Perhaps eighty yards left of the right end of
the crag is a glaringly obvious corner crack.

1. 40ft (12m), (5a). From the ledge climb
the fine corner crack with increasing difficulty.

Grooved Slab (Summary)

Over to the left again, past the wide easy
gully which provides a convenient means of
descent for both routes, there is an attractive
area of slabby rock. This is situated before
the crag begins to steepen and get really
green. Start near the left end of the slab.

1. 11m(35ft), (4a). A few easy ledges are
crossed to gain a groove. Climb this to a
mantleshelf at the top. Transfer left to a
shallow groove and climb it until a move left
or a move right leads to a ledge. (The ledge
on the right leads to the top of the descent
gully.)

Flake Crack and Grooved Slab (Description)

For me route names that accurately and
succinctly describe the climb they identify
have an endearing quality. Flake Crack and
Grooved Slab are the purest state of this
particular art and both offer excellent climbing to boot. However, before I describe
either, sadly neglected Helsby deserves a
few extra words.

When Helsby was in her prime, actually a
period spanning some forty years, she re-
ceived the attention of the greats: Colin
Kirkus, Jim Birkett, Hugh Banner and Al

Grooved Slab and its descent.

O belay point

descent

Grooved Slab

Rouse to name a few all left their indelible stamp on the crag. Not surprisingly the climbing is bold and demanding, and it has developed a reputation for difficulty and seriousness.

Although the rock is not above suspicion, with the advent of modern protection, Helsby on a dry day is a much pleasanter place to climb than its early reputation would suggest. On a damp or wet day however, the combination of moisture and chemical pollution, reputed to issue from the plant on the plain below, seems to clothe the crag in a jacket of luminous green.

Yet despite all this, when the evening sunshine beautifully bathes the soft red sandstone, there is ample reward to be found here and the two routes selected exploit all its best qualities. On a dry day too, the lichen does not effect either Flake Crack or Grooved Slab—indeed the whole of the right hand section remains relatively clean.

Take your large Friends and brute strength on Flake Crack and you will get perfect protection where you need it most. Take only a keen sense of balance and trust in your ability on Grooved Slab for I don't think you will find much else in the way of security. Take care, watch the roller bearing sandstone particles sticking to the feet, and have a good day.

Colin Matthews beginning the final difficult layback section of Flake Crack.

Trevor Jones in the groove before the mantleshelf on Grooved Slab.

CRATCLIFFE TOR: Fern Hill.
Map Ref: SK 228623.
Guidebooks: *Rock Climbing in the Peak District* by Paul Nunn. *Derwent Gritstone* by British Mountaineering Council.
Attitude: Faces south east.
Altitude: 700ft (220m).
Rock: Gritstone.
Access: Leave the A6 between Bakewell and Darley Dale to follow the B5056 south for some two and a half miles. A widening of the verge provides ample parking space and at this point the top of the crag is just visible over to the right (west). A track is followed through the fields which leads past a house and into a wood directly by the end of the crag. Note however that THIS IS NOT A RIGHT OF WAY. Keep to the track that veers off to the left and when this reaches the wood, walk along its inside edge to find the crag (15 minutes). The land is private but access is not prevented so long as the short cut across the field is NOT taken.
Observations: The crag itself is not named on the map but is marked Hermit's Cave. This is in fact scooped into the left end of the crag. It is one of the most pleasant of the Peak crags, and one of the higher grit edges, which although situated in woodland is generally light and airy. The rock is compact and of good quality.

Launching across the hard traverse of Fern Hill; the feint line of white chalk rises diagonally up the impressive vertical wall.

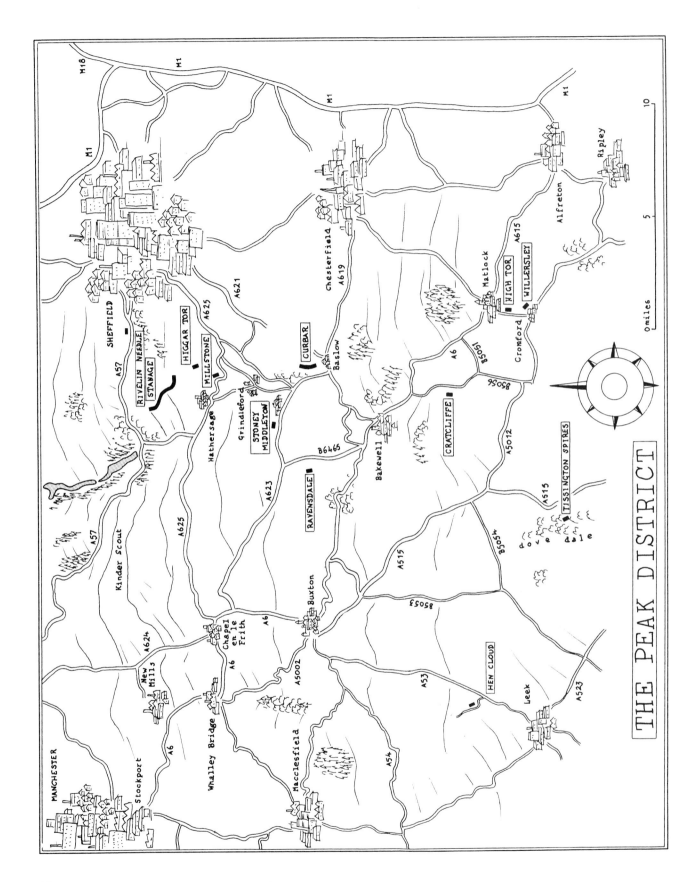

THE PEAK DISTRICT

CRATCLIFFE TOR: Fern Hill

FERN HILL: 60ft (18m), E2 (5c).
First Ascent: Peter Harding, Vin Ridgeway, (*circa* 1951). Nut for aid, Keith Myhill (1971). Free ascents followed shortly after.
Location: Left wall of the V-cleft, Cratcliffe Tor, central Peak District.

Fern Hill (Summary)

Past the Hermit's Cave (situated on the left end of the crag) is a broken jumble of rocks. Right of this the crag picks itself up and there is a distinct V-cleft. The left wall of this holds a crack leading boldly out left to the edge. This is the line of the climb. Start half way up the gully at the horizontal crack.

1. 60ft (18m), (5c). Finger traverse left with the crux moves made to reach the diagonal crack. Once gained follow this, through steep ground, to reach the blunt nose. Move up this to the jutting roof and move over to gain a final corner scoop leading to the top.

Fern Hill (Description)

The refined wooded situation combined with a fine tall cliff of excellent grit make this a remarkably pleasant place to climb. Proof that these qualities were recognised even in antiquary comes in the shape of the medieval Hermit's Cave to be seen on the left hand end of the crag. Although no records have survived this period, it would not be unreasonable to expect that a few scrambles at least were undertaken.

In fact mild controversy seems to surround the actual first ascent of Fern Hill. It was first recorded in 1971 when a point of aid was used and this was quickly dispensed with. Later Peter Harding claimed he had climbed a similar line in 1951. Exactly how Harding climbed it I don't know, and whilst as a matter of form I think that the first person to actually record an ascent should be accredited with it, if gritstone pioneer Peter Harding says he climbed the route then that's good enough for me.

Past the jumbled gully there is a distinct

O belay point

Fern Hill

Fern Hill on Cratcliffe Tor.

V-rift with a notably proud sheet of grit forming the left wall—a sheer face seamed with interconnecting horizontal and diagonal cracks. Linking the cracks to find a possible way up the vertical maze is the task undertaken by Fern Hill. The result is a hard climb of impeccable character.

The crux is a technical hand traverse, with the toes smearing the holdless vertical wall below, to gain a rising diagonal crack. A bold line across a steep and otherwise blank wall. However, despite the fact that the cracks look particularly round edged, it is a hidden feature of Cratcliffe grit that sharp edged finger holds are to be found. Protection too is right there where you want it.

You don't have to wait long before the sun rounds onto the climb. Any green emanating from the cracks soon dries to reveal the subtle reddish colour of the rock. There can be days when it is almost too hot for this climb. When I photographed Alison

Hargreaves, ably belayed by Ian Parsons, the heat was so intense that the chalk powder spiralled vertically upwards every time she dipped her bag. Not much fun when sweaty hands make it even harder to lock the tiny holds. Yet ultimately exciting when you gain the blunt nose to sense victory.

*Right: **Alison Hargreaves starting the crux hand traverse on Fern Hill.***

*Below: **Cratcliffe Tor, one of the highest gritstone outcrops, towers above the trees and cottage.***

PEAK DISTRICT—CURBAR EDGE

CURBAR EDGE: Peapod.
Map Ref: SK 258753.
Guidebooks: *Rock Climbing in the Peak District* by Paul Nunn. *Derwent Gritstone* by British Mountaineering Council.
Attitude: Faces south west.
Altitude: 1000ft (300m).
Rock: Gritstone.
Access: A minor road rises from the A623 through the village of Curbar. Follow this (the edge is plainly visible on the left), until after a distinct hairpin bend, some laybys appear. From here the path leads over a style and steeply up the hillside until a level track, situated just below the summit of the edge, leads to the Eliminates Wall. The line of Peapod is unmistakeable (8 minutes).
Observations: A very pleasant edge on which to climb, one most noted for its famous cracks. The southern end proves to be one of the most easily accessible in the Peak. Although high and exposed, the climate generally seems kinder on this edge than elsewhere and the gritstone is immaculate.

O belay point

Peapod

Above: **Once the pod is gained, whether to face left or right is the question.**

Right: **Peapod on Curbar Edge.**

CURBAR EDGE: Peapod

PEAPOD: 60ft (18m), E1 (5b).
First Ascent: Joe Brown, Slim Sorrell (1951).
Location: Eliminates Wall, southern end of Curbar Edge, central Peak District.

Peapod (Summary)

The peapod is situated left of centre between two other distinct cracks. Start up the thin crack leading into the pod.

1. 60ft (18m), (5b). The crack is immediately awkward to start but leads in a few feet to the pod. Climb the pod (facing left) to exit onto the small ledge on the right. Continue steeply up the crack and wall above to the top. Boulder belay a little way back.

Peapod (Description)

The presence of partially completed circular millstones shaped from the mother rock, can be found scattered along the approach track—tell-tale signs hinting at the formative origins of this edge which are confirmed when you arrive at the clean cut face of Eliminates Wall. Quarried or not, the gritstone found here is for many, the most satisfying climbing medium in England, and in the evening light, when the predominant soft brown colour is heightened to its fullest, the attraction becomes irresistible.

To the left lies the crack of Left Eliminate (a real struggle) and to the right Right Eliminate (even more desperate) but centrally the pure aesthetic line of Peapod has long symbolised the essence of Peak gritstone climbing. Little wonder that in its formative years, when the activities of Joe Brown, Don Whillans and the Valkyrie Club shaped the future of rock climbing, Curbar became known as 'The Cloggy of the Peak'. Cloggy being of course the climber's name for the huge Clogwyn du'r Arddu (The Black Cliff) on Snowdonia—one of Britain's largest and most formidable cliffs.

You may notice that the overall grade I have given to the climb, E1, is harder than that traditionally assigned to the route. I don't wish to enter the endless grading arguments but simply state that this grade is what I feel the route to be. But does it really matter? After all, when you are on form, there are really only two grades of route—those you can do and those you can't.

Starting the thin crack is a shock and it is no automatic procedure even to reach the pod. Many prematurely concentrating their minds on the anticipated difficulties ahead have rude awakenings here. Once reached, however, it is most surely the pod that holds the main interest.

To face right or to face left—that is the question. The right side is pretty much vertical but it does offer a high slit pocket foothold and the promise of a good handhold at the top, whereas the left side is smoothly arched, to give the peapod effect, and offers very little in the way of positive holds. But the apparent ledge hold on the right, the shelf that emanates from the top of the pod, is rather deceptive. Arguably the best way is to handjam the back of the pod with your shoulders and back on the right wall and feet running up the left to make most of the ruggosities which provide the vital friction.

That is the way I did it, although I have seen it done the other way. In either case the jams are pretty good and today the crack can be stuffed with the smaller sized Friends (sizes 1-2). More fool you if you hang about for too long placing them. Better, much better, to get one good placement at a reasonable height and press on with the climbing. Keep the rhythm flowing and the ascent will feel smooth and satisfying—break it for too long and you will surely pay a price.

You sense when you swing out right to stand on the ledge, that you have cracked it, and although steep above, only those completely drained of energy (a condition not unknown at this point), will err now. A brilliant exercise in jamming and off-widthing technique making perhaps the single most definitive statement about the art of gritstone climbing.

PEAK DISTRICT—HEN CLOUD

HEN CLOUD: Bachelor's Left Hand.
Map Ref: SK 008616.
Guidebooks: *Rock Climbing in the Peak District* by Paul Nunn. *Staffordshire Gritstone* by British Mountaineering Council.
Attitiude: Faces south west.
Altitude: 1, 150ft (350m).
Rock: Gritstone.

Access: Driving from Buxton to Leek on the A53, after about eight miles, a road leads off right near the bottom of a long hill, through the compact village of Upper Hulme and on beneath the castle-like mound of Hen Cloud. (Just along the road the more continuous edge of the Roaches can be seen.) At the conifer planting is a wide verge which provides parking and a distinct track leading directly to the crag (5 minutes).

Observations: An airy crag in a commanding position with simple access. There are many good lines and the rocks here are often quieter than the nearby Roaches. The Roaches and Hen Cloud are often referred to as the finest crags on gritstone.

Hen Cloud is a 'castle in the air'–like crag. The climber in the centre can be seen starting Bachelor's Left Hand.

HEN CLOUD: Bachelor's Left Hand

BACHELOR'S LEFT HAND: 80ft (25m), Hard
Very Severe (5a).
First Ascent: Don Whillans (*circa* 1957-61).
Location: Right face of Hen Cloud,
Staffordshire, south west Peak District.

Bachelor's Left Hand (Summary)

To the right of the broad gully a wall of grit
composed of distinct buttresses, rises sheer
from the ground. The last clean buttress at
the lowest point before the wall rounds the
corner holds this climb. Start near the left
end of the buttress some way beneath an
obvious crack that emanates from a sloping
shelf.

1. 80ft (25m), (5a). From a difficult and
immediately awkward start, move onto a
sloping break. A long reach into the crack is
made. Move up this (Friend protection)
until a reach rightwards gains a finger flake.
Move right on this (delicate footwork required), until a further sequence of moves
culminating in a mantleshelf, leads boldly
up to the ledge of Bachelor's Climb. (Possible belay here.) Move precariously into
the wide crack and follow it awkwardly to
the top.

Bachelor's Left Hand (Description)

The castle-like rocks of Hen Cloud are
perched romantically right on the top of the
hill. Unusually for the Peak they seem
distinctly independent—more like the buttresses of a mountain crag than those of a
grit edge which are more commonly found
stretched along the rim of a plateau. They
remind me in some curious way of the
magnificent Stac Polly in the high North
West of Scotland.

The route, the product of Don Whillans
at his peak, is right at the top of the grade
given here and despite modern protection,
still rewards the bold fluid approach.
Reaching the shelf and the crack is hard but
the meat lies above. The crack is now
extremely well protected but its position, on
the front face of this slightly bulging buttress, remains remarkably exposed.

*Bachelor's Left Hand: the leader can
be seen belayed below the final crack
with the second moving up just above
the crux.*

○ belay point

Bachelor's
Left Hand

Don may have had a pebble threaded with a sling to prevent him hitting the deck here but I don't expect he ever felt he really needed it. Today you launch off onto the crux with sound protection in place. This is difficult, perhaps just in the 5a technical category, and when you move from the crack to a finger flake hold high on the right, the footholds disappear and you are firmly committed to a bold series of moves first rightwards and then upwards.

After this you reach the ordinary route and it is possible to belay. It makes for a sustained pitch should you press on (and with modern rope management most will choose to), for entering and climbing the wide chimney above is still interesting. The moves completely contrast with the precision wall climbing below and it is a fitting end to an elegant route.

Funnily enough the first time I climbed the route it was behind Chris Bonington—a situation not without irony, for as Whillans had moved from state of the art rock climbing to the big mountains, here was Chris back from the big hills onto the rocks.

He made a steady determined lead, with frequent comment: 'Christ—this is typical Whillans.' I could tell he was enjoying it when he elected to continue bypassing the possible belay at the junction with Bachelor's Climb. And enjoyment is what it's all about isn't it?

A climber high on Bachelor's Left Hand.

PEAK DISTRICT—HIGGAR TOR

HIGGAR TOR: The Rasp, The File.
Map Ref: SK 255819.
Guidebooks: *Rock Climbing in the Peak District* by Paul Nunn. *Stanage Millstone* by British Mountaineering Council.
Attitude: Faces south.
Altitude: 1, 250ft (380m).
Rock: The roughest Millstone Grit in the Peak District.
Access: Situated on Hathersage Moor a little way above Hathersage. A road leads from the A625 at Hathersage Booths to wind directly below the outcrop. Alternatively the outcrop can be reached directly from Sheffield following the road through Ringinglow to take the right fork at the junction beyond Burbage Rocks. There is parking on the verge and a track, via a stile over the fence, leading to the top of the rocks—this is just a little way up the hill and not at the point the road passes directly below the rocks (5 minutes).
Descent: An easy climb leads into the gap at the back of the block.

Observations: The climbs described here are situated on the main section which takes the form of a huge tilted block. Despite any slightness in height the angle of the main face, taken by The Rasp, makes for unforgettable climbing and keeps the rock dry even during heavy rain! The rock is of first class quality and offers a remarkable vista and situation as fine as any in the Peak. There is much bouldering of considerable variety either side of the main block.

The Rasp and The File on Higgar Tor.

HIGGAR TOR: The Rasp, The File

THE RASP: 60ft (18m), E2 (5b).
First Ascent: Joe Brown (1956).
THE FILE: 40ft (12m), VS (4c).
First Ascent: Don Whillans, 1956.
Location: The central leaning block of Higgar Tor, northern Peak District.

The Rasp (Summary)

Start left of centre of the overhanging main wall.

1. 60ft (18m), (5b). Gain the flake and layback up until a move right (thread) allows entry to a shallow groove. Climb this crux until stopped by the final overhang. Traverse awkwardly right to make a finish up the short chimney leading to the top of the block. (The direct finish is bold and 5c.)

The File (Summary)

The right end wall of the block contains a fine crack.

1. 40ft (12m), (4c). Jam the crack.

The Rasp and The File (Description)

The Rasp and The File; Joe Brown and Don Whillans are names synonymous with gritstone and with much that is best in British climbing. The Rasp was for a long time regarded as the hardest route on grit and solving the problem of this grossly overhanging wall remains a technical masterpiece offering one of the most elegant and strenuously sustained pieces of climbing to be found on gritstone. The File so typically Whillans (no messing, directly to the point), is a line so blatant as to be immediately classic. One of THE jamming cracks. What a legacy this pair have left for rock climbers to enjoy. Their list of routes, stretching throughout the length and breadth of Britain (and on to the Alps, the Himalayas et al), climbed both together and individually, almost defies comparison.

The central block of Higgar Tor seen in profile, even from some considerable distance, presents a disturbing image. It

Strenuous climbing and a long way to go on The Rasp.

doesn't look possible that it should lean so much without either sliding down the hillside or toppling over. Close acquaintance does little to dispel its alarming aspect. The block does look perfectly stable, but the tremendously overhanging face offers no easy options for those intent on scaling it. The Rasp takes the face full on whilst The File cuts the end wall on the right.

In many respects The Rasp reminds me very much of another Joe Brown classic: Bow Wall on Bosigran in Cornwall gently overhangs in similar fashion and on both it strikes one that Brown must have been particularly inquisitive to stretch his neck along these continually strenuous and imposing pieces of rock. Despite the explosive power required even to leave the ground, perfect cool control must be exercised from the onset for there is no respite.

Plenty of excellent protection is available today, including at the time of writing an insitu thread, but anything utilised requires a measured amount of energy to hang on and place. An interesting equation evolves: whilst protection may be infinitely plentiful the climber's strength and energy are not. Neutrality is not acceptable and at some point the individual knows he must press on and make more physical and mental effort or fail.

The hardest bit, when perhaps you feel you have had quite enough pain already,

Higgar Tor showing the great tilted block with climbers on The Rasp.

defies any rational climbing style—a vague groove, a vital hold where you least expect it—so the best advice is simply to apply the gritstone 'udge' and keep moving up employing friction and faith if nothing much else. Finally, below the top an overlap overhangs unmercifully. You can go straight over, but this is seriously hard; efforts to exit right find most people forcing head and arms into the horizontal break. Despite the skin-grating results and arm-pumping stre-nuosity ebbing the final remnants of strength from abused forearms, these last few frustrating feet must be endured to complete a tremendously sustained piece of climbing.

Despite unsuccessful attempts to climb The File over a twenty-year period and a growing reputation of impossibility resulting in it being dubbed 'Vicious Crack', one cannot really imagine Don Whillans finding any difficulty with it at all in 1956. His Goliath for example, a similarly striking line on nearby Burbage South climbed in 1958, still rates an E4, 6a grading. However I'm equally sure this absence of extreme difficulty wouldn't have worried Don. For although he was mostly associated with hard climbing and hard deeds, in truth the grade of his climbs would always take second place to the quality of the line. The File is a perfect jam crack, perhaps petite but pure in ethic from bottom to top.

The nature of The Rasp is clearly revealed in this picture.

Halfway up The File.

PEAK DISTRICT—HIGH TOR

HIGH TOR: Darius.
Map Ref: SK 298590.
Guidebooks: *Rock Climbing in the Peak District* by Paul Nunn. *Peak Limestone South* by British Mountaineering Council.
Attitude: Faces west.
Altitude: 650ft (200m).
Rock: Limestone.
Access: This most impressive face of limestone dominates the narrow dale between Matlock and Matlock Bath. It is clearly observed standing directly above the River Derwent; parking may be obtained in two laybys situated either side of the iron bridge crossing the river to the 'Heights of Abraham' cable car station. Cross the bridge to the cable car station from where a path leads up the wooded hill. Some stone steps may be found and then a horizontal track which contours around the steep hillside to give access to the foot of the crag (15 minutes). The grounds are private and a fee may be charged on entrance or by those running the café at the top of the crag. Alternatively it is possible to park on the top at the café car park and pay a fee. Access is then an abseil over the cliff (a bush on the edge at the highest area marks the top of Darius) or by the usual walking descent (see below).

Descent: From the top of the main crag walk right to a natural terrace that leads down via some hand rails. At the bottom of these, bear right to descend steeply through the trees to the path traversing back to the foot of the crag.
Observations: Very much the showpiece of Peak limestone, this is a magnificent crag of excellent rock. Although the grounds are privately run, access is not a problem although a small fee may be charged. There are currently plans for development with the intention of restoring the grounds and gardens to Victorian splendour. Apparently climbing will not be adversely affected.

Darius on High Tor.

HIGH TOR: Darius

DARIUS: 160ft (49m), E2 (5c).
First Ascent: O. Woolcock, C. Rowland, P. Nunn (November 1963). Reduced to one bolt for aid, E. Ward-Drummond, T. Proctor (January 1971). Free, P. Livesey (1974).
Location: Main Face High Tor, south Peak District.

Darius (Summary)

Starts approximately in the centre of the face at a little groove 50ft (15m) left of the large distinct slanting groove (this is Original Route HVS).

1. 30ft (9m), (5a). Climb the surprisingly awkward little groove to a shattered horizontal break.

2. 130ft (40m), (5c). Step left from the belay and climb the bulge to gain a groove. Continue up this until another groove on the right, containing a good crack, can be gained. At its top the crack flattens to produce a large flake (this sounds hollow). Stand on this to pull up and then traverse diagonally rightwards to an old peg (a belay can be taken here). Traverse left to another groove and up this to break out onto the right wall. Climb directly up to make a long reach to clip the bolt runner. Step down slightly then climb diagonally leftwards utilising small finger holds (crux) to gain a shallow groove. Continue to the overhang and move right to break through it (jugs) to gain a short corner leading to the top and tree belays. (Small bush to the left on the edge and monster trees directly behind some distance from the edge).

Darius (Description)

It takes little imagination to understand why High Tor is acclaimed as the finest sweep of limestone in the Peak District. Any motorist driving along the A6 below can't fail to register this sheer face. It is shudderingly impressive. Completely vertical, totally unbroken, its main wall, taken by this climb, consists of clinically white rock. Increasing the dramatic visual effect, the left end of the wall steps out in a series of overhanging bulges with the rock, where the water weeps, colouring to soot black.

Richard Wright on the wall of Darius with the bolt runner visible.

There are no easy climbs here. Some aspirant ascensionists are psyched out without even leaving the car, and it's no place for the timid. But this great cliff is seldom really wet unless it is actually raining, and like most pieces of rock it turns out to be much friendlier on closer scrutiny. So bite the bullet and enter the Lion's Den by getting up there and inspecting the wall from its foot.

If you are climbing the grade then Darius is one of the very finest offerings. A full frontal route of some elegance with sustained climbing and a technically interesting crux. Individually the moves are absorbing and following one after the other, as they are here for some 160ft (49m), produces a powerful climb.

Carry a comphrehensive rack of gear (nothing ultra big) because the climbing is fortunately well protected throughout. Even the initial groove is decidedly awkward but this is just a warm up for the big pitch ahead. This starts with a bang and continues in much the same vein but, keeping it within the grade, good rests can be had at reasonable intervals.

An old peg marks what was once the belay, but a stance here is a pretty dismal affair and most will continue. Left into a groove, up and out onto the right wall and then some reachy moves to clip the bolt. This is placed high (the particularly short have been known to preplace a sling on abseil in order to reach the clip), and protects the finger sequence of moves leftwards. These constitute the crux and some thought should be given to getting the order right. Once decided, it is too steep to linger; positive commitment is required.

The route could be described as consisting of a series of grooves each presenting their own problems. Whilst the climbing and linking of each is quite different there are two outstanding common denominators. The unrelenting angle and the quality of climbing. In Darius both combine to make one of the most satisfying climbs on Peak limestone.

Alison Hargreaves below the final overlap of Darius.

PEAK DISTRICT—MILLSTONE EDGE

MILLSTONE EDGE: Great North Road, London Wall.
Map Ref: SK 248803.
Guidebooks: *Rock Climbing in the Peak District* by Paul Nunn. *Stanage Millstone* by British Mountaineering Council.
Attitude: Mostly faces west.
Altitude: 100ft (300m).
Rock: Millstone Grit.
Access: The edge runs north from the Sheffield to Castleton A625 on the hill just above Hathersage. Before the top of the hill beneath a rock cutting, a rising track runs due north from the road. Park at the entrance to the track (don't block it) or on one of the many spaces on the hillside below. Walk up to or along the track passing first an opening on the right (containing the Keyhole Cave Area) to gain entrance to the main quarry (The Embankment), higher up (5 minutes).
Observations: The Edge is the product of extensive quarrying. Generally the walls are straight and clean and often set togther at precise geometric angles to produce bold arêtes. Early climbing was extensively peg aided and this resulted in widening and cleaning many of the cracks to a comfortable finger width. Despite these rather dubious sounding origins the rock and the climbs are superb. There is a considerable density of fine climbs and the main problem here is one of selection. The Edge is exposed and can be cold on windy days but when the sun shines on the crag, in the early afternoon and evening, Millstone can provide a tremendous climbing experience.

As the evening sun lights the crag, the leader nears the roof overhang of Great North Road.

MILLSTONE EDGE: Great North Road and London Wall

GREAT NORTH ROAD: 115ft (35m), Hard Very Severe (5a).
First Ascent: Joe Brown (*circa* 1957). Previously pegged by P. Biven, T. Peck.
Location: Entering the quarry the most obvious feature over to the left is a very clean wall containing some straight cracks—The Embankment. Left of it is a great corner, the biggest in the quarry, and this is the unmistakeable line of the route, Millstone Edge, central Peak District.
LONDON WALL: 70ft (21m), E5 (6a).
First Ascent: John Allen (*circa* 1975). Previously pegged by P. Biven, T. Peck
Location: This lies on the far right wall of this section of quarry and is situated at right angles to the main walls (faces north), Millstone Edge, central Peak District.

Great North Road (Summary)
Start beneath the corner.
   1. 115ft (35m), (5a). Climb the slab and cracked wall until possible to move right into the corner itself. Climb the crack and impending corner above to pass the roof and gain an easier rift leading to the top.

London Wall (Summary)
The line is the obvious peg-scarred crack.
   1. 70ft (21m), (6a). The sustained and bulging crack leads up and left to a vague rest before the commiting final section leads on to the top. There are usually a couple of pegs to clip en-route.

Great North Road and London Wall (Description)
For their day, both these routes constituted significant breakthroughs in both attitude and difficulty. Joe Brown led Great North Road free at a time when it was predominantly the norm to peg up the cracks at Millstone. John Allen made a finger searing lead of London Wall to produce a technical masterpiece significantly harder even than its hard contemporaries. Both are glaringly

Great North Road on Millstone Edge.

John Clayton moving from the roof into the crack on Great North Road.

London Wall: Passing the midway point to make the big effort up the finger searing crack to the top.

obvious challenges and remarkable climbs yet there the comparisons must end. A considerable spectrum of difficulty separates the two. Great North Road has a big route feel to it with the hanging wall that forms

the corner impressing its presence on your psyche. It is all too easy to feel that you can't do it even before you start. However it genuinely does give reasonable climbing within the Hard Very Severe grade and is a

quality route with lots of impact even if it is no pushover—a hallmarked Joe Brown climb.

Within a few feet the steepness makes itself apparent and very soon you feel a

O belay point

London Wall

London Wall on Millstone Edge.

sense of exposure. Holds are good and so is protection, but confidence is the keynote of a successful approach. You must keep moving but quite a few of the moves are far from easy though easy to get wrong if you rush them without some thought. Once the corner itself is gained, a bold approach is required to reach and surmount the roof. Frequent Friends are most welcome, and considerably relieve the anxiety (imagine it with only a few jammed grit chocs for protection). But be careful. Do not place them too deep under the overhang as it is possible for the drag of the rope to walk them in here—a few battered aluminium skeletons bare testimony to this.

My Polish friend Jan Fijalkowski was over to experience something of the British rock climbing. The famous London Wall was on his hit list of routes. The fact that conditions were freezing and the north wind howled relentlessly meant nothing to this veteran of the cold north faces. So we had to go. It was pure purgatory. I refused to even put my boots on; my frozen hands would have been almost incapable of fastening up the laces. Jan cracked the bottom bulging section and battled on to half way before, after hours of struggle and with fingers stripped of skin he eventually conceded that conditions were not suitable. An amazing performance.

The peg-opened crack is perfect for the finger ends and this explosive route is one requiring a high level of finger power, good technique, stamina as it is remarkably sustained with only a semi-rest just over the half way point, and a committed approach to keep going up the final section of crack when the footholds run dry. Not many (Polish men excepted), would tackle it in conditions less than favourable. Everything has to be going for you to make a clean ascent of a route of this calibre.

One advantage of the wall is that it is pretty easy to stand back from the rock and work out the rack of gear you should carry. Perhaps the first overhanging section is the most strenuous and difficult but the climbing is fiercely sustained. The top section rewards the bold approach, although visualising the finishing sequence of moves is recommended before you start, and completes a very fine test piece.

PEAK DISTRICT—RAVENSDALE

RAVENSDALE: Medusa.
Map Ref: SK 173737.
Guidebooks: *Rock Climbing in the Peak District* by Paul Nunn. *Peak Limestone Stoney* by British Mountaineering Council.
Attitude: Faces west.
Altitude: 980ft (300m).
Rock: Limestone.
Access: From the A623 Stoney Middleton to Chapel en le Frith road, some 3 miles out of Stoney turn left to the village of Litton. Turn left out of the centre to follow a narrow road for some miles. Keep left at all the junctions

until, after passing narrowly through some houses, the road begins to zigzag down a steep hill. After the largest elbow there is a small road on the left (acute manoeuvre required when approaching from this direction) a little way before the bottom of Cressbrookdale is gained. A few hundred yards along this there is a parking area before a tiny street of cottages—Ravensdale Cottages. From the parking area a path leads down the field over the stepping stones and directly up to the large crag (7 minutes).
Descent: The descent path (shortest and

best way down) lies over to the right of the crag.
Observations: A crag of some size, placed perfectly to receive the afternoon sunshine, situated in a most attractive and quiet dale. As would be expected, the sight is an important one from a natural history point of view and is owned by the Nature Conservancy Council. Whilst climbing is not restricted in any way it is particularly important to stick to the marked paths and minimise your effect on the environment.

Medusa on Ravensdale.

RAVENSDALE: Medusa

MEDUSA: 150ft (46m), Very Severe (4b).
First Ascent: D. Johnson, D. Mellor, 22nd May 1960.
Location: Raven Buttress, Ravensdale, Peak District.

Medusa (Summary)

The path meets the crag at its lowest point and this climb starts just left of this behind a little tree.

1. 60ft (18m), (4b). A crack leads to a broken-looking wall above. Climb this and then move right to belay in the distinct rift crack formed by a large pinnacle.

2. 90ft (28m), (4b). Take the crack to stand on the pinnacle. The gangway groove above is climbed until finally it is possible to transfer leftwards and across into a distinct groove leading to the top.

Medusa (Description)

Left of the dominant Raven Buttress (the large central prow that makes up the most impressive part of Ravensdale), lies a distinct clean-cut gangway groove hewing leftwards. This is the climb described here; an attractive line fitting comfortably into the mid Very Severe category. But a word of warning must be given. Despite the popularity of the route one can never completely trust the blockey limestone holds. However the constant additional concentration required to deal with this factor adds yet another dimension to the climbing interest.

One of the major attractions of climbing the rocks of the Peak is the contrasting environment in which they are to be found. The exposed edges standing above the endless desolate moor, the quarries cleanly cutting the hillside or sunk into the ground, the startling white faces above busy main roads and here, situated in a quiet secretive dale occupying a commanding position above olde worlde cottages and deciduous woods, a natural limestone buttress of impressive stature.

Andy Blaylock moving right to the pinnacle stance on Medusa.

The autumnal day we decided to tackle the route started in dreary fashion. Clinging wet mist rolled leisurely through the trees highlighting weird forms and dampening enthusiasm. So back to Stoney café. Then a few rays of sun grew and it was thought a chance may develop. Indeed it did. Back in the dale as we crossed the polished stepping stones those self same weird trees began to shine in unbelievable hue. As all the colours of autumn smiled it was impossible to find fault with her charm or the challenge of the sunny white limestone rearing vertically upwards from the steep hillside.

Medusa beguiles you. The initial flake crack looks charmingly simple but is a lot steeper and more demanding than you would think from below. Still that is no bad thing and to compensate that deception there is another. The scrappy looking wall that leads you up to gangway isn't really scrappy at all.

The gangway groove is the reason for the route and the rock here is like white marble. The climbing is exhilarating consisting of curiously sharp edge hand holds and offering polished sponge fossils for the feet. A little water weeping from the groove provides further interest but this route whisks away left avoiding the ferocious-looking hanging corner groove directly above. That is Via Vita and yields at a much harder technical grade of 5b. Some thought should be given to the ropework, for the pitch is a big one and it moves some way leftwards across and into the final groove—by which time the leader is out of sight and often out of hearing of the belayer below.

Freddie Snallam and Andy Blaylock, who had climbed The Nose of El Capitan three weeks earlier, completed the route and brought me up to the strains of 'Big Bad Bill'. The sun shone and an old gentleman in the cottage gardens below lifted his stick in acknowledgement of the ascent. There was no traffic noise to be heard.

Looking through the miniature street of Ravensdale cottages to the crag towering above.

PEAK DISTRICT—RIVELIN NEEDLE

RIVELIN NEEDLE: Croton Oil.
Map Ref: SK 278873.
Guidebooks: *Rock Climbing in the Peak District* by Paul Nunn. *Stanage Millstone* by British Mountaineering Council.
Attitude: Faces south.
Altitude: 820ft (250m).
Rock: Gritstone.
Access: Whilst there is no right of way, the owners do not mind climbers so long as the following access route is adhered to. The Needle and the Rivelin Edge behind actually fall within the Sheffield City boundary. It is usual to park by the side of the A57 immediately by the lane that leads across the top of the lower Rivelin Dam. On the opposite side of the A57 to the dam a track leads to the left end of the edge. Before the edge bear right to find the Needle (5 minutes).
Descent: Abseil into the gap behind the Needle.

Observations: Despite the approach being somewhat akin to a jungle in midsummer, Rivelin Needle is a prominent feature standing cleanly on the hillside. Situated below the edge it commands a handsome view (particularly attractive during the autumn fall), across to the Rivelin Reservoirs. Although the rock (fine-grained grit) is sound, it does become a little green after rain.

Trevor Jones belayed on the top of Rivelin Needle.

RIVELIN NEEDLE: Croton Oil

CROTON OIL: 65ft (20m), HVS 5a.
First Ascent: Dick Brown, Donald Wooler, Frank Fitzgerald with five points of aid (March 1952). Free Pete Crew, Oliver Woolcock (1963).
Location: The southern face of Rivelin Needle, beneath Rivelin Edge, Sheffield City, Peak District.

Croton Oil (Summary)

In the centre of the downhill, south, face of the Needle there is a short wide crack leading to a ledge. Whilst one may start up this it is more attractive to walk round onto the ledge and begin the climb from this.

1. 65ft (18m), (5a). Balance up the wall moving diagonally leftwards passing the thin cracks (good runner in the highest). Make a long reach up left to the flake crack and launch up to gain the ledge on the shoulder (the notch). Take the hollow-sounding flake above to gain the summit.

Croton Oil (Description)

There were many attempts to climb this evocative pinnacle from the earliest days of Peak climbing but it didn't finally fall until 1932 when a rope was thrown over the top to safeguard the ascent. Croton Oil took a little longer to climb but it was worth the wait, for it is the most natural and enjoyable route; one that is doubly blessed by both excellent climbing and the means to reach the summit.

It's quite surprising that within a few yards of leaving the busy A57 (the famous Snake Pass road from Sheffield to Manchester), you feel that you are in wilderness country. Rivelin Edge and Needle are not so popular as other grit edges and the path leading through the woods below can become a veritable jungle of thorn, briar and bracken during the summer months. Despite the ensuing battle the solitude will be welcomed by many and the Needle itself is whistle clean, placed higher on the hillside with a commanding view. It's a most obvious challenge and it is hard to believe it was climbed so late in the day; it should be on the list of all aspiring Peak climbers.

Trevor Jones climbing on Croton Oil.

abseil descent

O belay point

(route obscured)

the notch

Croton Oil

The rock is fairly fine grained and, despite the southerly aspect, tends to remain rather green after rain. Nevertheless, friction is good and the route can certainly be done in damp conditions—as Trevor Jones so ably demonstrated to me one drizzly November day.

From below, the difficulty of the climb is not easy to assess. The strategically placed thin cracks provide the inspiration, but it isn't easy to rationalise the distance between them. Will you be able to make the span and reach from one to the next? Well there are reaches to be made but technique will make up for any deficiencies in height—for principally, the main problem is one of balance.

The objective, the notch—a ledge on the shoulder—is obvious enough but a steady approach will be re-paid rather than a vigorous attack. After the initial wall, a horizontal break is reached on the left and moves to stand in this provide food for thought before a thin diagonal crack and good runner on the right offer some sense of permanence. Reaching a flake crack high on the left provides the next challenge. In the right crack, downward strain on the fingers that secure you to the face must now be reversed. Push must replace pull. Great stuff—technically-demanding gritstone climbing requiring reasoned technique. Despite the distance it is worth taking the flake crack as high as possible. What's the crack like? Well if it wasn't as good as it is, the grade would be significantly higher, for the ground remains steep until the sanctuary of the notch is gained.

A little care should be taken above this for although a flake gives good holds it does sound distinctly hollow. However, a few feet only remain to the top and a short abseil from a mutitude of insitu slings. Time now to admire your position and reflect on the absorbing intricacies of this elegantly demanding adventure.

A long reach gains the best part of the crack on Croton Oil.

STANAGE EDGE: Black Slab, Left Unconquerable, Right Unconquerable

Map Ref: SK 245834 to 226865.
Guidebooks: *Rock Climbing in the Peak District* by Nunn. *Stanage Millstone* by British Mountaineering Council.
Attitude: Faces west.
Altitude: 1, 400ft (430m).
Rock: Millstone Grit.
Access: This major edge is situated above Hathersage and runs south to north along the plateau of Hallam Moors. It can be reached from a number of points along the A625 or directly from Sheffield through Ringinglow its southern end. Ample parking on the roadside just below the road junction, provides access to Black Slab. The well trod path leads diagonally up past the first buttresses (Black Hawk Area and Flying Buttress) to reach the distinctive wall of Black Slab in a few hundred yards (10 minutes). Further down the hill there is a marked car park (nearest to the southern end of the edge) partly shielded by trees, and this provides the access point for the Unconquerables. The path leads up to a little wood where the path bears right to emerge from the wood with the routes just a little way further (15 minutes).
Observations: This is the most major gritstone edge in Britain. Stretching for four miles it attains a height of 50ft (15m) in places and offers an unparalleled feast of grit climbing with over 500 climbs to choose from. Although it dries relatively quickly it occupies a very exposed position, often blasted by wind and rain. It is also perhaps the most popular crag in Britain and although teams can be found in action throughout the year the further one ventures from its most accessible southern end the less busy it becomes.

Looking north along the full length of Stanage Edge; there are many climbers in action despite the snow.

STANAGE EDGE: Black Slab

BLACK SLAB: 50ft (15m), HS (4a).
First Ascent: A. T. Hargreaves (1926).
Location: Black Slab Area, Stanage Edge, northern Peak District.

Black Slab (Summary)

Start in the centre of the slab.

1. 50ft (15m), (4a). Step leftwards onto the centre of the slab then climb directly until a traverse leads across to the left edge. Follow the edge until it is easier to traverse back right, to finish more or less directly. Note the above description is the easiest way up the slab and there are many variations possible. Hargreaves' Original Route (VS, 4c) climbs the slab directly up the centre.

Black Slab (Description)

It was J. W. Puttrell, as long ago as 1890, who first realised the rock climbing potential of Stanage Edge. There were no crowds in those days but there were problems. Climbs frequently ended in conflict and there were many vociferous running battles with gamekeepers who had been primed to keep their masters' grouse moors intact. Various cunning means were employed to overcome these little difficulties, including bribing the aforesaid with barrels of beer, but today the areas described here are owned by the Peak Park Planning Board and access does not present any problems.

There is no doubt that, as the sun sinks towards the moors rising again to the west and the soft browns of the grit begin to redden with the sky, Stanage Edge is a remarkably genial place to be. But for the climber it is the rock that will be found to be all absorbing and of the very many excellent climbs to be found the majority are steep, often quite brutal, and few refrain from coming directly to the point immediately hand touches grit. The most notable exception to this rule, and all the finer for it, is Hargreaves' Black Slab.

This slab requires a different art. Fine balance, a steady approach, and a measured understanding of the rock's characteristics are the essential leader qualities. Moving

A climber nears the top of Black Slab as the light begins to fade.

confidently between the breaks, utilising the pockets, maximising the ruggosities, flowing along the line of least resistance; this is the climbing craft to be employed here.

There isn't much protection, although with all the modern devices I'm sure some could be found. But much of the satisfaction of this route is climbing without needing it. There are places where it steepens and you must carefully judge just how best to use the feet, there are places where handholds disappear, and there are times when you realise that 20ft, 30ft, 40ft and 50ft is a long long way to be above the ground and that the particular line you follow must be within your particular capabilities. In 1929 Hargreaves climbed it direct at a technical grade of 4c without runners. You can too if you choose to or you can weave a little with the rock and decipher a way that suits you best. This is a route on which to take off the blinkers and reap the rich rewards of self assertion.

Incidentally it is cold comfort to know that the great pioneer Alf Bridge, in the early 1930s, is reported to have taken controlled falls from near the top of Black Slab; dropping and sliding for some 50ft to land painlessly uninjured. Quite bizarre—I don't recommend you try this potentially fatal subsport. However Alf Bridge wrote:

'Most of my practice falls were off gritstone climbs in Derbyshire, and more often still did I have one or two practice nights a week in a quarry not very far from my home.

'It depends on the type of pitch as to which falling methods I use. For instance, if I am on a slab I deliberately flatten myself against the rock and friction my way down to the stance. In another instance I may be on a broken face of rock, and in that case I should try and decide very quickly which is my best landing place and jump. But in both these instances I must land with my feet together and relaxed muscles, and quite prepared to roll myself into a ball and not fall backwards on to my head.

'I think that guts and coolness are the most important parts of the technique to develop.'

Being more than a little crazy would help too. 1929 was a breakthrough year on Stanage and this route played a significant part of a push in standards that embraced Kelly's Overhang, HVS 5b, and Christmas Crack, HS 4b, (the attractive and distinct crack just right of the Black Slab). A. T. Hargreaves, as did many of the other pioneers involved in that period of development, moved on to make a significant contribution to Lake District climbing. In doing so, he helped establish that now often

belay point

Black Slab on Stanage Edge.

quoted fact: that the sound and varied climbing techniques, learnt by necessity on grit are capable of taking one to the highest levels of achievement on rock anywhere.

The best times on Stanage are those when you are at the top of your form and climbing continuously without the fetters of rope and slower companions, and when the days stretch long into the night. Not too long ago the Robin Hood's Caves, just left of the Black Slab, provided climbers with a free roof for the night, but much of that solitude and freedom has disappeared with the huge increase in popularity of the sport. However, despite the crowds, I'll wager much of the best climbing will still be discovered when you're out front on the Black Slab.

1. June 1932 *Mountaineering Journal*—'The Technique of Falling' by Alf Bridge.

STANAGE EDGE: Left Unconquerable and Right Unconquerable

LEFT UNCONQUERABLE: 50ft (15m), E2 (5c).
First Ascent: Tom Probert, Albert Shutt (*circa* 1949).
RIGHT UNCONQUERABLE: 50 ft (15m), E1 (5b).
First Ascent: Joe Brown, Slim Sorrell, Wilf White (*circa* 1949).
Location: Unconquerable Cracks Area, Stanage Edge, northern Peak District.

Left Unconquerable (Summary)

Start up the obvious crack.

1. 50ft (15m), (5c). The leftward slanting crack is found to be overhanging and the overlap at the halfway point provides the crux.

Right Unconquerable (Summary)

Start at the same point or more directly with a noticeable increase in the technical difficulty.

1. 50ft (15m), (5b). The obvious layback flake crack is usually gained from the left, starting as for the previous route then following the horizontal break right to the flake. (The direct start is somewhat harder.) Layback the flake cracks until below the overhanging top block, this is the crux and is tackled directly.

Left and Right Unconquerable (Description)

Two traditional routes epitomising all that is best about gritstone crack climbing. Hard, tough, rugged and honest, success in climbing them requires the fearless dynamic approach; an approach not only demanding a degree of physical strength and mental commitment but one balanced with a determined fluidity and subtlety of technique.

The seventeen-year-old Joe Brown cruised them both, beginning the legend although unknown to Brown Tom Probert had actually succeeded on the Left Unconquerable before him. Ironically, and appearances are deceptive, it is this route that is the harder of the two. And, as many have found, significantly so.

Left and Right Unconquerable on Stanage Edge.

belay point

Right Unconquerable

Left Unconquerable

The grit of Stanage is not quite the roughest in the Peak but it does offer substantial adhesive qualities. And as any experienced gritstoner knows, despite the muscle power required to make upward progress against the grain of the rock its roughness will always reward thoughtfully reasoned footwork; a physical quality that it is essential to exploit on these two routes.

The initial bottom crack of Left Unconquerable is straightforward enough despite its rather alarming impending nature but the good times end in an overlap just over halfway up. The moves here look innocuous from below—and later on as you critically analyse the moves in the pub no one move will appear particularly difficult—but in-situ, with the crux to climb, things may appear different. The pure physical difficulty of hanging on will occupy much of your efforts. Yet beyond this physical dilemma you will need the mental push to launch into harder moves with a long reach left to pass the overlap. Above, the steepness rises unabated but the holds get much bigger. The pull over the crevassed block on top really is no problem and with physical effort diminished, thought once again can be directed at the aesthetics of style should there be any punters you would like to impress with the effortlessness of it all.

Aesthetically, in execution and being, the Right Unconquerable is the better route. Hanging flakes—round edges sculpted by the eons of wind and weather—form the perfect challenge. The direct start is a boulder problem in itself and one should not feel too bad about starting over to the left and traversing back to the flakes. In any case, the character of the route lies above this point. Protection is as good and frequent as you want, with the crack taking large Friends, but take care not to place them too deep. On my last visit there was a neat new rock scar on the bottom edge of the flake. Apparently a Friend had been jammed and someone had broken the rock to remove it; an act of desecration.

The technique: layback, hands and feet, pull and push, equal and opposite, all harmoniously balanced yet committed to upward movement. Ingenious; the climbers answer to verticality. There must be no doubts, and to get the maximum from the route, keep the protection placements to the minimum, feel the freedom of confident movement as you work up the first flake to holds and then back right into the steepness of the crack and up to the final block jutting out above your head. The crack stops here and the direct pull over the top is the crux. It always ends ignominiously, grovelling on the flat holdless top, pretending to mantelshelf. Nevertheless, with the route completed, the feeling is a good one, of a great piece of climbing having been executed; of soaring with eagles in the kingdom of Baron Brown.

Topping out in style on Left Unconquerable.

Andy Blaylock using friction for the feet on the second layback flake on Right Unconquerable.

STONEY MIDDLESTON: Sin.
Map Ref: SK 223758.
Guidebooks: *Rock Climbing in the Peak District* by Paul Nunn. *Peak Limestone Stoney* by British Mountaineering Council.
Attitude: Generally faces south west.
Altitude: 560ft (170m).
Rock: Limestone, highly polished in places.
Access: The crag is situated immediately above the main road at the west end of Stoney Middleton. Just out of the village there is a sizeable parking area on the left and it is best to leave vehicles here. Shortly after a garage on the right, a track leads into the woods and continues beneath the white prows and walls of Windy Buttress. Over to the left of this stands an independent pinnacle of rock—this is the Tower of Babel (5 minutes).
Observations: Stoney dries quickly after rain and is well situated to provide all-year-round climbing. Ease of access and the café just down the road ensures the massive popularity of the crag. Although the sheer volume of humanity can be frustrating on occasions the convenience and quality of the climbing provides ample compensation.

Fred Snallam nearing the top of the final groove on Sin.

STONEY MIDDLETON: Sin

SIN: 100ft (30m), Very Severe (4c).
First Ascent: Ron Moseley, February 1952.
Location: Left side of the pinnacle known as The Tower of Babel, Stoney Middleton, central Peak District.
Descent: The most straightforward descent is probably to abseil down the left bay of the tower from the notably stout tree. However this may not be wise if parties are climbing below because any dislodged loose rock would seriously jeopardise their safety. The best alternative is to move back into the jungle and bear right to pick up the descent from the Windy Buttress routes. Continue right contouring the top of the buttress (care not to descend prematurely) until a well-worn gully leads down the far right end of the buttress.

Sin (Summary)

Start from the trees on the left side of the pinnacle. There are two distinct groove crack lines above and this route takes the right-hand one.

1. 100ft (30m), (4c). Climb the rather friable barrier wall to the horizontal ledge (alternatively—the original way—climb the chimney on the left to reach the horizontal ledge). Move across to gain the right-hand groove crack and climb this steeply using a combination of jamming and bridging. A horizontal break at about mid height does not prove unwelcome.

Sin (Description)

You really couldn't describe Stoney as aesthetically beautiful. The cliff, a strange mixture of natural and man-scarred limestone consists of rock that varies from interesting to downright scary, although the hazards of it being loose are now arguably surpassed by that of it being polished. Stone dust and the noise of heavy traffic and machinery permeate from the working quarry situated opposite and from the main road below. Yet there is something endearing about the place, especially when the sun shines and the green mantled trees screen much of man's activity.

Sin: The Tower of Babel seen through the bare trees on a winter's day.

48

Certainly activities here have been the influential touchstone of the development of limestone standards in the Peak District. From Tom Proctor to Jerry Moffat, before and beyond, bold statements of just what is possible on rock have been made here. Then there is the cafe, a perfect place to dodge the wet, glean information and pysche up for rock that dries immediately the rain stops.

It may appear hard to select one route from a hot house of development and it is. But one of the earliest adventures, Sin, can be singled out to exemplify its grade. Originally given Exceptionally Severe, presum- ably because of the psychological pressures generated by the unknown stability of the great pinnacle—The Tower of Babel—it now lies at the top end of the Very Severe category. Being a climb of some interest and yet somewhat tucked away from general view, it manages to retain an air of dignity.

I have described a way directly up the barrier wall which is not how it was originally climbed. You can go up the chimney to the left, in traditional manner (and the rock is a lot better there) but climbing the wall shortens the traverse right and helps with the ropework. In any case it is the splitting corner groove that provides the keynote of interest.

This is Very Severe Peak limestone climb- ing at its most rewarding, being both steep and difficult enough to make you glad of the excellent protection that can be placed. It is sustained to a degree that when a resting combination of foothold and hand jam does occur, you take it willingly; it offers a corner of verticality, that makes you jam, bridge and think about just how best to use the flinty nodules; it is absorbing to a degree that you quite forget the awesome possibil- ity of the tower moving.

Stoney Middleton: early morning light illuminates Windy Buttress (right) and the finger-like Tower of Babel on the left.

PEAK DISTRICT—TISSINGTON SPIRES

TISSINGTON SPIRES: John Peel, George.
Map Ref: SK 521146.
Guidebooks: *Rock Climbing in the Peak District* by Paul Nunn. *Peak Limestone South* by British Mountaineering Council.
Attitiude: Faces south.
Altitude: 1, 050ft (320m).
Rock: Limestone.
Access: Tissington Spires are situated in Dovedale and can be reached by walking from either end of the valley although the walk from the north at Milldale, is probably the more interesting even though the longer of the two. The A515 Buxton to Ashbourne road provides the main access to either end. Follow minor roads to Milldale and continue through the tiny village to find a large car park (just past a field car park where a charge is made). Walk back through the village to cross the tiny arched stone packhorse bridge and on beside the river. A little over half way, by a wooden bridge, the distinct finger of Ilam Rock points skywards. Keep on going until Reynard's Cave is passed on the left, after which the trees disappear to reveal the Tissington Spires above (just past a little ruined pumphouse by the side of the track). Although the distance is only around two miles allow about 30 minutes for there is much to see. If you walk from the southern end, follow the Ilam signs from Ashbourne car park (fee charged) beneath the Izaak Walton Hotel. Keep up the valley past the stepping stones and Tissington Spires appear as the first major rocks above on the right (20 minutes).

Observations: Leafy Dovedale is renowned for its considerable beauty (see *Classic Walks In Great Britain*) and holds much of interest to the rock climber. The many features are too detailed to mention here but the two routes selected on Tissington Spires provide climbing of considerable character. Tissington Spires consist of thin blades of limestone running at right angles to the river. The south wall of the central blade provides the site for the climbs chosen.

The central limestone reef of Tissington Spires where John Peel and George lie.

TISSINGTON SPIRES: John Peel, George

JOHN PEEL: 165ft (50m), Hard Very Severe (5a).
First Ascent: P. Williams, J. H. Amies (1964).
Location: On the main wall looking over South Gully, Tissington Spires, Dovedale, southern Peak District.

Descent: Abseil.
GEORGE: 130ft (40m), E1 (5b).
First Ascent: Climbed as an aid route by S. Read, R. Leeming, D. Carnell, P. Brown, S. Hunt (1956). Two points of aid P. J. Nunn, J. Morgan (November 1969). Free in 1970.

Location: Left side of the main wall overlooking South Gully, Tissington Spires, Dovedale, south Peak District.
Descent: Down the broad easy gully, South Gully, to the right.

Mike Mortimer belays Marjorie Mortimer up the final awkward section of the ramp of John Peel; it is advisable to abseil off here.

The leader reaches the crack which leads magnificently up the final wall of George.

John Peel (Summary)

This is the line of the large curving corner. The corner groove is gained from the right by traversing in from the gully. Start some way up the gully.

1. 165ft (50m), (5a). Traverse left and move up to the corner. Follow this traversing right beneath the bulges to a ledge (possible stance). Move up to the right and follow the ramp with some difficulty to reach the yew tree belay. It is best to abseil from here.

George (Summary)

Left and lower than John Peel is a shallow groove, start up this.

1. 130ft (40m), (5b). Take the groove, which proves awkward, to gain a corner and overlap with a peg runner above. Move out left, with a step down, to cross the exposed wall and reach a further peg runner on the front. Continue directly up the crack to the top.

John Peel and George (Description)

The rock fangs of Tissington Spires offer much more continuous climbing than is suggested by the head-on view from the valley floor. Despite the fact that both these routes start from the bed of a gully they rapidly give a sense of exposure. George in particular climbs some sensational ground and looks most improbable.

Nevertheless, the difference in difficulty is not that far apart: the final ramp of John Peel can be particularly hard, certainly at the very top of its grade, if attention is not given to careful footwork, whereas it is the innocuous initial groove (particularly if the rock is damp), of George that may provide unexpected difficulty, despite the extreme looking nature of the ground above.

If the initial corner groove of John Peel should weep then an alternative start may be taken up a groove to the right (actually the start of climb called Black Flip). Although steeper, necessitating the surmounting of an overlap to gain the wall before the ledge on John Peel, the climbing is comparable to the true start. The stout Yew tree gives a short abseil into the steeply plunging gully and is by far the best way to get off this climb, the rock above being broken and extensively vegetated.

By the time you make a leisurely start and enjoy the walk either of these climbs provide sufficient entertainment to fill a climbing day, although should you wish to do both then John Peel gives the gentler introduction, along with a good view of the intricacies of George. Whatever strategy you choose you will discover two splendid routes perfectly in tune with this heartland of the White Peak.

O belay point

John Peel

George

easy gully

John Peel and George on Tissington Spires.

PEAK DISTRICT—WILLERSLEY CASTLE CRAG

WILLERSLEY CASTLE CRAG: Pothole Wall.
Map Ref: SK 297570.
Guidebooks: *Rock Climbing in the Peak District* by Paul Nunn. *Peak Limestone South* by British Mountaineering Council.
Attitude: Faces north.
Altitude: 295ft (90m).
Rock: Limestone.
Access: Approaching south along the A6 from Matlock, the crag is to be spotted on the left side of the road (just after Matlock Bath) and immediately before the Cromford road junction, where a track leads off through distinct iron gates and runs directly below the crag. Note there is no parking allowed here and vehicular access is strictly forbidden, so drive a few hundred yards further on, bearing left and a short distance away there are two large parking areas on the right of the road. The church gate opposite leads to the far end of the track seen earlier. It leads directly below the crags (5 minutes).
Observations: The crag consists of a continuous wall of limestone liberally bedecked in vegetation and shrouded by trees. Despite this greenery and the fact that the crag faces north, it is peculiarly sheltered and often provides a climbing venue when rain stops play elsewhere. Indeed, it is quite often one of the best climbing choices for a winter's day in the Peak.

Jane Billingham approaching the first stance of Pothole Wall.

WILLERSLEY CASTLE CRAG: Pothole Wall

POTHOLE WALL: 130ft (40m), Very Severe (5a).
First Ascent: S. Read, B Jackson (1959). Free D. Hadlum, D. Gray *circa* (1960s).
Location: Pothole Wall Area, Willersley Castle Crag, south Peak District.

Pothole Wall (Summary)

Nearer right than centre, a right-facing corner, right of a large tree, marks the start of this route.

1. 70ft (21m), (4c). Move up the corner and climb an overlap. Follow the groove above until stopped by overhanging rock and ivy above. Move steeply left and climb the rib to a ledge. Climb up the short corner above, moving diagonally leftwards to a stance with rotting pegs and better nut belays.

2. 60ft (20m), (5c). Move up and right to the obvious hole and insitu threads. Step down and move right across the wall to gain the edge (crux and is often damp when the rest of the route is dry but it is well protected). Move back left above the roof to gain the groove which leads directly to the top.

Pothole Wall (Description)

On first aquaintance one could be forgiven for describing this crag as rather scraggy; an afterthought of a climbing ground; a place to go when all else has been done. This impression is heightened in summer when for most of its length it is hidden by a thick green canopy and cradles a multitude of

Moving right from the Pothole is the technical crux, but it is very well protected.

luxuriant growth amongst its folds.

But after the route has been climbed, after breaching the hundred-foot-plus limestone wall, solving its intricacies to rest on the whaleback top and view the River Derwent and Willersley Castle beyond, its elegantly refined character will out. The Castle was built by a father figure of the industrial revolution—Sir Richard Arkwright in the late eighteenth century. Today it is a methodist religious centre and hotel. They own the crag as well, and whilst they permit climbing they do appreciate a quiet approach.

The wall is vertical but seamed regularly with well defined, if somewhat disjointed, vertical grooves and corners. These provide the main climbing lines and offer predominantly clean wholesome limestone. Of course care with the holds, taking nothing for granted, must always be exercised with Peak limestone—even on the Pothole Wall.

If the first overlap were placed a little higher and in a more spectacular position, rather than just a few feet off the ground, it would most probably constitute the crux. Situated as it is though, it is usual to dismiss any difficulties experienced as merely warming up blues. The defined groove above proves entertaining until it can be quitted by bold moves left onto the very steep rocks of the rib. Fortuitously the holds are always good enough to maintain the standard within the Very Severe category. Even so, the difficulties are sustained with the climbing stretching unbroken from the ground right up to the stance.

Above to the right hangs the wall containing the hole and it is quitting the fissure to cross it that provides the recognised technical crux. Countering the fact that this is often wet from water oozing from the presumed subterranian caverns above, it only takes a single move pass it. An impressive position now greets you with much air rushing straight down below your feet but the protection is immaculate.

There is more steep climbing ahead and concentration must be maintained until the friendly tree belays can be taken on the top. Even if the winter hot aches (the painful effects of blood flow being restored to chilled limbs) should temporarily paralyse the hands and maim the mind at this point (as they have done to me so many times), the warm afterglow of satisfaction makes it more than just a worthwhile climb.

Pothole Wall on Willersley Castle Crag.

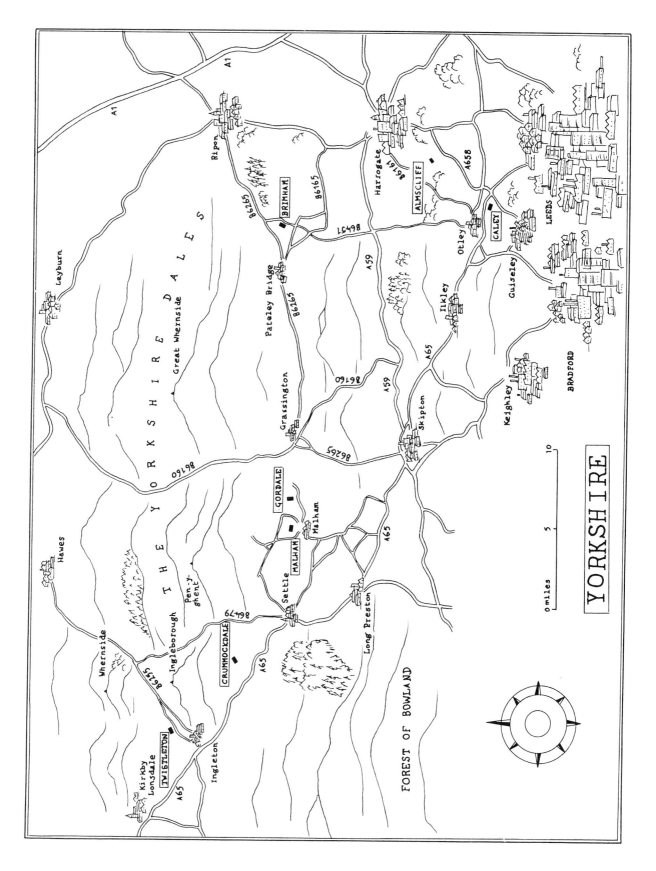

YORKSHIRE

0 miles 5 10

YORKSHIRE—ALMSCLIFF

ALMSCLIFF—Great Western.
Map Ref: SE 268490.
Guidebooks: *Rock Climbing in Northern England* by Birkett & White. *Yorkshire Gritstone* by The Yorkshire Mountaineering Club.
Attitude: Faces west.
Altitude: 500ft (150m).
Rock: Gritstone.
Access: A prominent high landmark, the rocks are situated conveniently close to the A658 about five miles south of Harrogate and ten miles north of Leeds. The nearest village is probably North Rigton and the road from here leads on past a farm to a wide verge and ample parking. A stile over the wall marks a path leading directly to the North West Face—the West Face is just around to the right (5 minutes).
Observations: Almscliff has long been the mecca of Yorkshire gritstone climbing and its importance as a climbing ground far outstretches its meagre 50 foot height. It is invariably strenuous but there is a tremendous variety of climbing and bouldering to be found. Because these summit rocks, consisting of various walls and tiers, virtually circumscribe the hillside there is generally something to climb in most weather conditions. However in recent times the farmer has used the rocks as a wintering ground for his cattle. Consequently the surrounding ground has been reduced to a quagmire so don't forget to take a cleaning towel.

Ian Dunn moving left on the famous hand traverse of Great Western. The climbing here is both strenuous and exhilerating.

ALMSCLIFF: Great Western

Great Western: 50ft (15m), Very Severe (5a).
First Ascent: Arthur Dolphin, 1943.
Location: North West Face, Almscliff, Yorkshire.

Great Western (Summary)

Just to the right of the normal point of arrival a pile of boulders forms the base of the crag as it shifts around to the west. A distinct corner and crack mark the start.

1. 50ft (15m), (4c). Climb the steep corner layback crack until a reach down left gains a horizontal hand traverse leading out left. The steep wall is crossed until a strenuous pull enables a pinnacle boss to be gained. Continue to jam up the steep impending groove until a pull out left. A short crack leads to the top.

Great Western (Description)

If one route could be picked out to epitomise all that is best about Yorkshire gritstone then this is surely it. Arthur Dolphin's proud route, Great Western, links a line of obvious weaknesses to take a sensationally exposed line up and through the uncompromisingly steep rock of the North West Face. The climb imparts an unforgettable blend of steepness and strenuosity—a heady northern brew unique to this gritstone crag of crags.

Arthur Dolphin started on these rocks as a schoolboy apprentice combining rare talent with a massive enthusiasm. After time served, he became a master craftsman, bold, innovative, competitive and strong. He fre-

The north-west face and surrounding rocks of Almscliff, seen from the approach path.

quently soloed this route, often in nailed boots, but even so, few climbers today will shun the protection afforded by modern equipment. They would be foolish to do so, for should strength begin to fail on this unrelentingly strenuous route there is little chance of success.

The initial crack sets the theme, yet the comfortable security it offers is brought to an abrupt end by the hand traverse left. From now on in it's all arms and confidence. A diagonal crack for the feet helps to launch the attack. Runners can be placed in the horizontal hand break (strength permitting), as you proceed, but at the end it is necessary to make rapid committment to quickly execute the hard pull into the steep shallow groove above. The pinnacle-like flake of grit does provide security but isn't really an apt place to rest, and soon the fight to the top must be recommenced.

Almscliff is often referred to as an outdoor gymnasium, as the nature of the rock dictates that all routes require a fair degree of physical fitness. Whilst this is an apt description, and for many the quality of climbing offered is an end in itself, on Dolphin's Great Western quality of climbing and character of line are fused. The result is a masterpiece.

Great Western on Almscliff.

O belay point

Great Western

YORKSHIRE—BRIMHAM ROCKS

BRIMHAM ROCKS: Minion's Way, Maloja, Frensis Direct, Allan's Crack.

Map Ref: SE 209637.

Guidebooks: *Rock Climbing in Northern England* by Birkett & White. *Yorkshire Gritstone* by Yorkshire Mountaineering Club.

Attitude: Generally the rocks face west (although this is not always so for the climbs described here).

Altitude: 1200ft (360m).

Rock: Particularly excellent gritstone, naturally sculpted into distinct blocks and towers.

Access: The rocks are situated on the moor above Summerbridge about 8 miles north east of Harrogate. The rocks can be reached by taking the steep hill up by the side of the pub in Summerbridge, or from the B6265 Pately Bridge/Ripon road. There is a large car park (National Trust—a small fee is charged) and access to the individual climbs will be described separately from here. In all cases the walk is never more than a few minutes.

Observations: The rocks consist of an amazing cluster of pinnacle towers and block boulders. Birch Tree Wall has already been featured in *Classic Rock Climbs In Great Britain* but apart from this fine climb, it is the varied nature of many climbs that make a classic outing on this unique area. I have therefore chosen a selection of routes, all quite short, that go to make up a classic climbing day on Brimham Rocks.

Jamming the cracks of Frensis Direct, strenuous and getting harder.

BRIMHAM ROCKS: Minion's Way

MINION'S WAY: 35ft (11m), Hard Very Severe (5b).
First Ascent: Allan Austin and Dennis Gray both climbed it independently on the same day (1957).
Location: Cubic Block west face, Brimham Rocks, Yorkshire.
Descent: A scrambling retreat from the top of the block is best effected by lowering to a lesser block on the south side and crossing the gap via a jammed boulder. Alternatively well polished climbs up the east face, around Severe in standard, can be reversed.

Minion's Way (Summary)

Walk west from the end of the car park and this distinctly large block will be found in a couple of minutes. The crack up the centre of the west face is unmistakeable.

1. 35ft (11m), (5b). Climb the short difficult crack to a sloping ledge. Continue up the wide impending corner crack to make an exit out right onto a sloping slab. A little wall leads to the very top of the boulder.

Minion's Way (Description)

A traditional Yorkshire gritstone Very Severe which I'm afraid I've had to regrade for the sake of justice! How many Very Severe leaders must have failed to leave the ground in days gone by—hundreds, thousands? There is a trick, of course. It's generally referred to as the jamming technique.

The way I do it is to take a low jam, this controls the body and enables the feet to be placed on ruggosites, before I reach higher for the obvious widening in the crack. The way **not** to do it is to stretch as high as possible and launch up regardless. But however you do it, the crack, once jammed, is extremely painful. If you are new to jamming remember that the best way to know if the jam is a good one is to look away from the crack and use the jam when it feels best.

This, the major technical difficulty is only short lived and once the horizontal ledge is reached the climbing becomes quite different. Although not so hard above, it is still brutal, forcing a way up the overhanging corner, and it now becomes scary as well. A very full route after which you cannot help recalling the age old grit adage:

Expert: 'You can always tell a gritsone climber by his hands.'
  Novice: 'Lots of scars?'
  Expert: 'No scars.'
If your hands remain intact after this particular route consider yourself an expert.

John White masters the painfully difficult hand jam start of Minion's Way.

Above left: **Nearing the cannonball hole of Maloja.**

Above right: **Martin Scrowson laybacking the fine corner crack on Allan's Crack on the Fag Slab area of Brimham Rocks.**

Right: **John White moving up the last few feet to the summit of Frensis Direct.**

BRIMHAM ROCKS: Maloja, Frensis Direct

MALOJA: 45ft (14m), Hard Severe (4a).
First Ascent: J. R. Lees (*circa* 1950s).
FRENSIS DIRECT: 40ft (12m), E1 (5b).
First Ascent: Allan Austin (1957).
Location: Cannon Rock east face, Brimham Rocks, Yorkshire.

Maloja (Summary)

From the car park take the track (low barrier to prevent vehicular traffic) for 200 yards or so until, beyond the trees/bushes on the left, Cannon Rock with its distinctive hole can be seen in a couple of minutes. The route starts from a ledge just left of the twin cracks.

1. 45ft (14m), (4a). Climb the shallow corner, scoop to gain some better holds then traverse left to the hole. From here ascend to the top.

Frensis Direct (Summary)

The obvious twin cracks up the centre of the east face of Cannon Rock.

1. 40ft (12m), (5b). Gain and follow the cracks from the cave to reach a bulge. Pull left into the overhanging crack above and climb to the top. Useful holds will be found on the prow to the left.

Maloja and Frensis Direct (Description)

There is little comparison in nature or difficulty in these two little gems but both polarise two specific qualities of gritstone. The former requires balance technique, disciplined footwork and the maximum utilisation of rounded semi positive hand-holds. The latter demands explosive power to transfer from already steep jamming to the even steeper rock above.

Even though Maloja is considerably easier than Frensis Direct it contains a short section of reasonably demanding climbing and, wrapped on either side, is sufficiently varied ground to make this an entertaining exercise. Frensis Direct is the test-piece; short but direct; highly worthwhile and wholly satisfying. If you can do it that is.

Maloja and Frensis Direct on Brimham Rocks.

(route obscured)

Maloja

Frensis Direct

BRIMHAM ROCKS: Allan's Crack

ALLAN'S CRACK: 40ft (12m), Mild Very
Severe (4b).
First Ascent: Allan Austin (*circa* 1955).
Location: Fag Slab Area, Brimham Rocks,
Yorkshire.

Allan's Crack (Summary)

From the car park walk along the track to
pass Brimham House (National Trust information centre and cafe). Continue in the
same direction on the path to pass the
distinct Dancing Bear Buttress and drop
down into the woods below the broken edge.
Continue along beneath the crags to cross a
stone wall. About 40 yards further on, the
Fag Slab ends with the prominent corner of
this climb. There is a distinct overhang at
mid height. Allow about 15 minutes from
the car.

1. 40ft (12m), (4b). Layback up the
corner moving left around the overlap, and
continue to a restrictive ledge above the first
overhang. Move right and finish up the edge
above. The slab left of the corner can be
climbed direct using the tiny pebbles—this
is harder but quite climbable.

Allan's Crack (Description)

A very elegant open route rewarding the
bold approach. The rock, albeit worn to a
polish in places, is superb and the position
exciting. The laybacking that takes you up
the corner to the break above the first
overhang is suitably protected with nuts and
this makes the route fairly amenable,
although a certain composure must be
maintained to select and place them effec-
tively.

The direct start up the slab left of the
corner, utilising the silica pebbles cemented
in the grit, is a totally different experience
and a definitive exercise in delicate footwork. Technically it is quite a bit harder
than the corner but if you have any energy
left after your full day on these superlative
rocks, both ways deserve a separate ascent.

*A climber moves out under the roof
of Allan's Crack.*

YORKSHIRE—CALEY CRAGS

CALEY CRAGS: Psycho, Angel's Wall, Roof Layback, Roof of the World.
Map Ref: SE 231444.
Guidebooks: *Rock Climbing in Northern England* by Birkett & White. *Yorkshire Gritstone* by Yorkshire Mountaineering Club.
Attitude: Generally the hillside faces north, but the individual routes selected face both east and west.
Altitude: 800ft (240ft).
Rock: Gritstone.
Access: The crag and boulders lie on the hillside above the main A660 Otley to Leeds road, about one mile south of Otley. Driving south out of Otley there is a wooden gate and wide verge with ample parking on the right side of the road. The routes selected are in different locations and individual access descriptions will be given separately for each.
Observations: This is thought by many to be the premier bouldering area of Yorkshire (if not Britain). Although there is an edge—some 50ft (15m) high—which constitutes the main cliff, and on which there are some notable climbs, I have opted to portray the classic character of the rocks by selecting a number of famous bouldering problems.

Dave Birkett top roping the difficult problem of Psycho.

CALEY CRAGS: Psycho

PSYCHO: 20ft (6m), E5 (6b).
First Ascent: Ron Fawcett (*circa* early 1970s).
Location: Roadside Buttress east face, Caley Crags, Yorkshire.

Psycho (Summary)

From the gate bear left for about a hundred yards or so to the lowest obvious large boulder. On the left side is a distinct pock-marked wall (Rabbit's Paw Wall) but round to the left of this and left of a deep rift is a smoother slabby wall. Psycho climbs the left side of this east face starting from a boulder some 15ft (5m) above the ground.

1. 20ft (6b). Traverse right, utilising a poor finger pocket, to gain the line of 'chicken heads' which lead directly to the top.

Psycho (Description)

You either solo or top rope this route for there is no natural protection to be found. Whilst in cold print twenty feet may seem a trifling distance for a climb, when you are out there on this particular piece of grit, it feels an awfully long and lonely way from the ground. To be strictly ethical it should be soloed on sight and this makes the route an extremely serious proposition. However it is an especially difficult route to 'psyche' up to, for although the climbing may only be short, you start from a position that is immediately too far above the ground to contemplate failure.

An interrupted line of vertical ruggosities provide the route's raison d'être. But the traverse right to reach these chicken heads (the nodules of grit that protrude from the clean slabby wall), is immediately hard and precarious. Once reached, the tiny but vital holds have to be used with precision. Straight cranking pulls alone will not suffice and advanced science, utilising both hands and feet, must extract the maximum from this line of vague possibility.

A route leading not only to the top of a grit boulder but to the summit is many a northern rock climber's ambition. Perhaps only a short climb for the accomplished—yet a considerable distance for the aspirant.

Dave Birkett stretching from the finger pockets to the chicken heads (pebble ruggosities).

CALEY CRAGS: Angel's Wall, Roof Layback, Roof of the World

ANGEL'S WALL: 20ft (6m), Very Severe (5a).
First Ascent: Arthur Dolphin (*circa* 1945).
ROOF LAYBACK: 20ft (6m), Very Severe (5a).
First Ascent: Probably Arthur Dolphin (*circa* 1940s).
ROOF OF THE WORLD: 10ft (3m), Very Severe (5a).
First Ascent: Probably Arthur Dolphin (*circa* 1940s).
Location: Sugarloaf Boulder east face and surrounding rocks, Caley Crags, Yorkshire.
Descent: The Sugarloaf is most easily descended by the rib to the left.

Angel's Wall (Summary)

Follow the track from the gate until an area of large boulders immediately above and below are discovered. The prominent boulder below is the Sugarloaf and the overhanging east wall visible to its right is taken by this climb.

1. 20ft (6m), (5a). Start from the right (although it is possible to move in from the left at an easier technical grade), and after a few feet, climb the wall centrally to a juggy finish.

Roof Layback (Summary)

Across the path and behind some other boulders, there is a large boulder with this alarming-looking line on its left side.

1. 20ft (6m), (5a). An impending layback crack leads up beneath an intimidating roof. Transfer to the rib on the left and finish up this.

Roof of the World (Summary)

Beyond this last climb to the west, amongst the jumble of boulders, is a prominent overhanging slab.

1. 10ft (3m), (5a). Climb the overhang using the awkwardly spaced horizontal holds. Feet are not allowed!

Dave Birkett in full flow on Roof Layback.

Dave Birkett gains the lip of Roof of The World.

Angel's Wall, Roof Layback and Roof of the World (Description)

Angel's Wall is the nearest of these to equate to a full route and certainly feels high for its meagre few feet. This is probably because the top overhangs even more fiercely than the bottom. The distinct advantage of this, not that I'm saying it rains much in West Yorkshire, is that the route, apart from the finishing holds, can often be found to be dry whatever the prevailing weather conditions.

Fortuitously it is the first few feet which constitute the crux and whilst grading is purely arbitrary, on a route of this length, I have called it Very Severe (5a) for historical reasons. Above, there is protection to be found, and if the route is led it should be sought despite the arm wrenching angle of dangle. Without it, a slip from the top would be very nasty indeed and the finishing holds, along with the rest of the boulder, can be luminescent green when this sheltered wall is quite clean and dry.

Equally remarkable move for move are the other two selected routes. Layback Roof yields to the bold, strong approach and the satisfaction of bursting out left onto the rib to clear the strenuosity far outweighs the size of the problem. Roof of the World had to be selected for the audacious name alone. To discover how a 10ft (3m) problem can be named so, just do it. But no feet. Start from a dead hang, no jumping, and keep on going up and down until the arms can't take any more. Then do it a couple more times!

With a little imagination, an afternoon's bouldering on the rocks of Caley Crags can equal in intensity a day's climbing anywhere. Indeed they provide the most varied bouldering in Yorkshire, but don't forget the towel and car mat to keep the mud off your boots. Well nothing's perfect is it?

Starting from the right of Angel's Wall is the hardest way and involves taking a high undercut to reach better holds above.

Dave Birkett silhouetted at the end of the roof of Roof Layback. The difficulty is now to exit up the rib.

CRUMMACKDALE: Venus.
Map Ref: SD 783704.
Guidebooks: *Rock Climbing in Northern England* by Birkett & White. *Yorkshire Limestone* by Yorkshire Mountaineering Club.
Attitude: Faces south west.
Altitude: 1000ft (300ft).
Rock: Limestone; care should be taken with the flakes.
Access: The crag lies on private ground and it is essential to obtain permission to climb from Mr Morphet of Town End Farm, Austwick. Simply telephoning Clapham 288 prior to your visit is all it takes to obtain this permission. The crag lies in the Crummackdale valley above the hamlet of Wharfe, which is in turn located just off the A65 some five miles north of Settle. There is parking on the verge next to a stream just before a barn. Just after this a private road leads up to the houses. Follow this through the farm, past the cottages and follow a track, past some converted barns and cottages, to find a lane that leads up the valley beneath the crag. A stile on the right leads to a field. Keep to the bottom of this field for a hundred yards or so until a further field provides open fellside to take you directly up to the crag. There is no need to climb any walls and permission is granted on the understanding that this is not done (25 minutes).
Descent: This is best over to the right of the crag (a stone wall contains a stile some 60 yards back from the edge of the crag). The wall that meets the crag is also crossed by a stile where the wall meets the crag.
Observations: The crag is noted for its rapid drying properties and despite its rather broken first impressions it offers some excellent climbing. It is not large, but high enough to provide longish one-pitch routes. Flakes, large and small must be treated with caution, although otherwise the limestone is of good quality. The crag developed a reputation for seriousness in the early days of exploration but with the advent of modern protection (small nuts and Friends are particularly useful), the climbing has become more amenable and it is a delightful all-year-round location in which to climb.

Tony Greenbank at the end of the traverse of Venus. A short flake crack leads directly up the steep wall.

CRUMMACKDALE: Venus

VENUS: 105ft (32m), Very Severe (4c).
First Ascent: Brian Evans, 1959.
Location: Crummackdale, Near Settle, Yorkshire.

Venus (Summary)

A stone wall meets the crag and the climb takes the curving slab line about 25 yards left of this. A flaky groove marks the starting point.

1. 105ft (32m), (4c). Climb the weakness to the slab and a small ledge. The overlap line leading out right is followed with some delicate footwork approximately mid way. Continue using the distinct undercuts to a vague corner where the overlap terminates. From here climb steeply to another little slab and then up a brief wall to the top. A number of belays should be taken.

Crummackdale (Description)

This climb is a good representation of the many available up the smaller limestone cliffs of the Yorkshire Dales. It may not be so grand and spectacular as those which can be found on the showpieces of Malham, Gordale or Kilnsey but it does have a character all of its own. Crummackdale too is a fine place to be. A wild dale, one giving a rich rugged feeling yet one also tempered with beauty of detail. A few trees, distinct crags and a contrast between high moor and low dale provide an atmosphere somewhere between that of Scotland and the Lake District.

Not that the fine views of high Ingleborough and distant Pendle Hill will absorb your attention for long, for once the climb is commenced you will be totally absorbed in its intricacies. At the start you still have to watch many of the flakes, but in general, after this the rock is remarkable: hard pin-pricked limestone giving noticeably good holding power to both fingers and boots.

Venus on Crummockdale.

O belay point

crux

Venus

The line is quite striking. A diagonal overlap, distinct on this crag of overlaps, leads markedly rightwards through the steepness. The overlap provides undercut holds for the hands, and the clean slabby wall below, a vital series of footholds. Undercutting, though an awkward rather unnatural technique, is effective and must be utilised here. All goes well until, about half way along the gently ascending traverse, the holds blank out. Here it is necessary to transfer the feet onto a higher slab and a specific sequence of holds must be selected and used with some precision.

It is a definite and precarious crux demanding total trust in foot friction, for whilst the footholds are suitably large, they slope disturbingly. Physically you will find that a balanced two-step movement overcomes the main difficulties. Psychologically it isn't quite that easy, for at this point the runners are some way behind you. The remainder of the climbing is smooth and clean, interesting and steep to the last, and runners can be placed more frequently.

Throughout, it is necessary to pay close attention to your rope work, extending runners where required, to prevent snagging and drag problems. All in all, Venus provides quite a long technical pitch and is a climb requiring a steady lead and a sound working knowledge of modern rope practice. A route at the top of its grade.

Tony Greenbank making the crux step-through right, on Venus; the undercut flake provides the handholds.

YORKSHIRE—GORDALE SCAR

GORDALE SCAR: Face Route.
Map Ref: SD 915642.
Guidebooks: *Rock Climbing in Northern England* by Birkett & White. *Yorkshire Limestone* by Yorkshire Mountaineering Club.
Attitude: Faces south east.
Altitude: 1200ft (360m).
Rock: Limestone.
Access: Turn right in Malham village over the little bridge and take the next junction right. Not far down this road a further bridge is crossed and there is parking on the verge and a signed path leading up the stream to the gorge (10 minutes).
Observations: Gordale Scar is actually a gorge deeply cut into the limestone. It is a fine sight and a famous tourist attraction. Care , therefore, should always be taken not to drop any loose rock without first checking no-one is below.

Graeme Livingstone moving up to the roof on the first pitch of Face Route.

GORDALE SCAR: Face Route

FACE ROUTE: 155ft (47m), E3 (5c).
First Ascent: Ron Moseley, Joe Smith (1956, climbed as an aid route). Ken Wood, Allan Austin (1971, 3 points of aid). Pete Livesey, John Sheard (1971, free).
Location: The gorge left wall, Gordale Scar, Yorkshire.

Face Route (Summary)

The approach path leads into the confines of the gorge and across the stream lies the left wall. An obvious corner, near the scramble ascent from the stream, marks the line of this impressive route.

1. 85ft (26m), (5c). Climb the corner to the often dripping roof. Move right, and continue directly up the wall to a shallow niche and resting point. Continue to a scoop above, with in-situ peg belays (treat with caution) and indifferent stance. (It may be wiser to continue a little way to good nut runners directly below the final roof.)

2. 70ft (21m), (5c). Move high, then traverse left to gain steep cracks which lead directly to the final roof. (A hanging belay can be taken at the bottom of these cracks allowing the second man a better view of the proceedings.) Move as high as possible up into the roof until a long high reach right reveals an excellent hidden hold. A short pull and a traverse right leads to a tree belay. It is usual to make an abseil descent from here.

Face Route (Description)

Face Route is a fierce and difficult adventure on Yorkshire limestone. Today there are many routes considerably harder, but even so this does not detract from the quality of climbing up this distinctly natural line of weakness. Adequate protection can be sought throughout, and if the first groove is wet, which is often the case, this will most likely be found to be the most difficult of the two—whatever technical grade you personally assign to each.

Controversy, the hallmark of many of Pete Livesey's early free ascents, hit the headlines in the early 1970s. Pete Livesey

Graeme Livingstone poised on the crux of the first pitch of Face Route.

and John Sheard claimed a totally free ascent of this audacious limestone route when many other top climbers had been forced to use aid. At that time it was a breakthrough in concept and by far the hardest undertaking on British limestone. It seemed unbelievable. To compound the doubts, eye witnesses alleged their style of ascent was far from the pure free ascent claimed by this upwardly mobile duo.

Today it is regarded as a regular hard limestone route, one full of character and action packed, but frequently climbed by those operating in the mid-extreme bracket. Indeed on a summer's day, as the swallows plunge through the gorge and the left wing melts in the sunshine, it is hard to care about the route's rather truculent beginnings. The climb ahead is all that matters.

For me it is the first pitch that is the hardest. Possibly this is because I have never found it dry. Every time I've been here a constant stream of wet has dripped from the overhang that tops the initial corner groove. In these conditions it is quite an art trying to keep at least one foot dry to make the friction moves right beneath the roof. And don't trust the pegs—they are mostly rotten.

The day I came with my cameras, despite the sun on the left wing, a cold wind still blew with some considerable keenness. This and the blackness on the other side of the gorge seemed to suck all heat away from the rock. But no matter, Graeme Livingstone had kindly agreed to lower his quite considerable technical standards to climb the route with me. After some months of intense bouldering on the granite boulders around Chamonix, the route was going to offer no contest to Graeme and I didn't therefore feel any guilt about asking him to hang about in photogenic places.

Consequently, when he had climbed the groove, in atrociously greasy conditions, and moved right onto what is arguably the technical crux and is in any case an exceedingly strenuous place to stop, I didn't hesitate to tie him off when he agreed it was, 'Good place to stop. '

There he hung, stretched between the distant holds and above distant runners as I went about my business. Nice to move, escape the wind, try different angles, bracket all the shots, change the film and leisurely return to take hold of Graeme's ropes again. Was that a faint muttering I heard as he resumed climbing safeguarded once more?

I honestly only realised his predicament

Face Route on Gordale Scar.

Graeme Livingstone preparing to move over the roof of the second cave on Face Route.

as I swung right from the overhang fighting to maintain my position on this vertical rock. I was stretched to reach the holds and I'm a good bit taller than he. Arriving at the stance (he passed the cave scoop to belay out in the cracks on the left) I said,

'I'm amazed you stopped just there but thanks anyway I got some good stuff!'

He replied fairly unenthusiastically: 'Thanks a lot Bill, I had difficulty reaching anything to hang on to and I couldn't pull any rope through.' (I had him well belayed to numerous anchors.) 'What I actually said was – no good place to stop here.'

Well you'd think he could have made the point a bit more forcefully.

His ascent of the next section and over the roof was forceful enough and he ended with the throw-away comment: 'That's never 6a.'

It is a considerable roof but protection is reassuring and if you get high under, and make a long reach up and right, the blind jug is amply generous. I'm not quite sure how Graeme reached it or even if he bothered to but I agreed that the move was nearer 5b than 6a and that the first pitch was significantly the harder. I had to really didn't I?

YORKSHIRE—MALHAM COVE

MALHAM COVE: Kirkby Wall, Wombat.
Map Ref: SD 897642.
Guidebooks: *Rock Climbing in Northern England* by Birkett & White. *Yorkshire Limestone* by Yorkshire Mountaineering Club.
Attitude: Faces south west and dries quickly.
Altitude: 1000ft (300m).
Rock: Limestone.
Access: Malham Cove is easily reached from Malham village where there is a car park and National Park Centre. Alternatively from the road that leads to Malham Tarn, to the east of the village, there is a widening of the verge (on a steep hill) and a signposted stile leads to the top of the Left Wing of the Cove (10 minutes).
Observations: Malham Cove forms a great horseshoe of natural limestone. In its centre it reaches a spectacular 300ft (91m); a rise of unbroken rock from the emerging stream to the final overhanging rim. The cove is a sheltered suntrap offering all-year-round climbing. Recently the advent of bolt-protected climbing has allowed a high density of routes to be forced and the central section has become one of the technically hardest climbing grounds in Britain. It is an extremely popular venue and now becomes plastered with brightly coloured bodies. However the Right Wing, from where I have selected the routes described here, still offers more traditional climbing of the highest quality.

The steep rib provides a testing start to Kirby Wall.

MALHAM COVE: Kirkby Wall, Wombat

KIRKBY WALL: 100ft (30m), Hard Very Severe (5b).
First Ascent: Allan Austin, Brian Evans (1961).
WOMBAT: 90ft (27m), E2 (5c).
First Ascent: Robin Barley, Dennis Gray (1964).
Location: Right Wing Malham Cove, Yorkshire Dales National Park, Yorkshire.

Kirkby Wall (Summary)

From beneath the central section, a path leads across the stream, diagonally rightwards to a large boulder beneath the Right Wing. This forms a useful place to picnic, view other climbers and to gear up. Start the climb more-or-less above this at a rib to the left of a shallow cave.

1. 50ft (15m), (5b). Start with difficulty then pull right, with help from a large flake, into a groove. Climb this until an awkward traverse leads left (it is usual to go higher and place a good runner below the roof before commencing the traverse), with a bush at foot level, to a ledge and belays.

2. 50ft (15m), (4c). Traverse left, upwards then downwards, to gain a ledge. Take the flake to a little corner then move out right to climb the steep wall. Pull out of this onto a glacis above and then up the short corner to the top.

Wombat (Summary)

Over to the left of Kirkby Wall a short vertical wall guards entrance to a prominent corner groove.

1. Climb the awkward wall to a tree stump much ravaged by passing climbers. Continue up the corner until this can be quitted by stepping right onto a sloping ledge. Continue to the overhang and pull rightwards over this to a corner groove. Up this until at its top a hand traverse leads left. Follow this until a long reach gains a further break. Pull up once more to a standing position in the highest break and continue with difficulty to the top by the fence.

Luke Steer chalks his hand before pulling up right into the midway corner groove of Wombat.

Luke Steer on Wombat, Malham Cove.

Kirby Wall and Wombat
(Description)

On Kirby Wall the high technical grade applies to the first few feet which are both steep and strenuous. After this the climbing becomes steady limestone Very Severe (4c). Even so, in wet conditions (and this route is often climbed thus), the polished footholds must be carefully selected and used. Although modern friction boots do much to counter the smoothness of the holds, the alarming undercut nature of the traverse left beneath the roof on the first pitch still demands careful consideration. Handholds assist balance only and footwork is crucial.

In many respects it is the second pitch that provides the most enjoyable climbing. It is not as difficult as the first, but it does bulge somewhat on the hardest section and a steady thoughtful approach is necessary to find the holds. Fortunately, although mostly hidden, they are there. And, as with many limestone routes, committment must come sooner rather than later for it is just too strenuous to dawdle.

Wombat is a climb of considerable quality, sustained throughout, yet reaching a crescendo right at the top. The bottom flakey wall (it used to be graded Very Severe in the true tradition of Yorkshire sandbagging) is constantly changing as the holds break off! Above this there is little in the way of loose rock, but much of interest.

Above the start, the corner wall and overhang lead into a final corner groove offering a little calm before the tempest breaks. At the top of this a flake crack takes some sound runners before the rounded break takes your full weight onto the front of the headwall. Steep moves gain a further horizontal break and from here it is necessary to gain a standing position. A small finger flake on the left and one on the right enable you to pull up, stand in the break and reach a strategically placed letterbox pocket. Yuk. Invariably it's full of glorious mud but you daren't let go before composing yourself for the final move.

The common denominator with all Yorkshire limestone climbing is that it is invariably steep and strenuous. Within that context the two routes chosen here provide as much contrast and variety as could be wished for. Despite any reservations you may have regarding the newly constructed footpaths, lines of shiny bolts with attendant admirers and coach loads of tourists, when the sun shines through onto the piercingly white rock of Malham Cove it is fine place to climb.

Kirby Wall and Wombat on Malham Cove.

YORKSHIRE—TWISTLETON SCARS

TWISTLETON SCARS: The Candle, Evening Star, Priority.
Map Ref: SD 716763.
Guidebooks: *Rock Climbing In Northern England* by Birkett & White. *Yorkshire Limestone* by Yorkshire Mountaineering Club.
Attitude: Faces south east.
Altitude: 1000ft (305m).
Rock: Limestone.
Access: The scar is situated a couple of miles out of Ingleton and can be easily seen from the B6255 Ingleton to Hawes road. It is located on the opposite side of the valley to Ingleborough and is reached by taking the minor road that runs on the north side of the river. There is parking on the open field verge at Twistleton House Farm directly below the crags. A small reasonable charge may be made. The crag is reached by walking up the field to a gate (do not climb over any walls or fences)—this sports a sign saying 'Strictly No Dogs'—which leads onto the open hillside. Continue directly until a defined track leads to the left side of the scar (8 minutes).
Observations: Despite any initial impressions regarding the height of the crag this is a remarkably pleasant place to climb. It has an attractive outlook, dries quickly and offers numerous entertaining climbs of excellent quality.

Tony Greenbank on the crux overhang of The Candle.

TWISTLETON SCARS: The Candle, Evening Star, Priority

THE CANDLE: 35ft (11m), E1 (5b).
First Ascent: Allan Austin (22 December 1963).
EVENING STAR: 50ft (15m), Hard Severe.
First Ascent: Tony Greenbank (5 January 1963).
PRIORITY: 65ft (20m), Mild Very Severe (4a).
First Ascent: Brian Evans (22 December 1963).
Location: Twistleton Scars, near Ingleton, Yorkshire Dales National Park, Yorkshire.

The Candle (Summary)

The Candle is situated on the left end of the crag, and right of the obvious break in the scar. The slim pillar has an obvious overhang some 15ft (5m) above the ground. Start up the thin cracks beneath the left end of the overhang (the distinct crack to the left is Candle Crack).

1. 35ft (11m), (5b). Climb steeply to the overhang (runners can be placed in the crack up to the left but it is very strenuous to do so). Move right to utilise the thin flake crack emanating from the right-hand side of the overhang and pull directly over onto the pillar above. Continue directly up the centre of the slim pillar without deviation to right or left.

Evening Star (Summary)

The corner above the large boulders that litter the path.

1. 50ft (15m). Gain a thin corner and

Tony Greenbank enjoying Evening Star, the climb he first pioneered many years ago.

Tony Greenbank in the delightful final corner groove of Priority.

○ belay point

○ belay point

The
Candle

Evening
Star

Priority

climb up this until better flake holds lead leftwards to a larger corner. Continue directly to the top.

Priority (Summary)

Round the prow to the right is another stretch of wall. Start roughly in the centre of this.

    1. 65ft (20m), (4a). Climb the awkward broken wall to gain the left end of a clean rightward sweeping slab situated half way up the crag. Follow the slab rightwards to ascend into a hanging corner. Continue up this to the top.

The Candle, Evening Star and Priority (Description)

The good-looking slim pillar of white limestone is a most striking line. But beware, it doesn't yield easily. Even leaving the ground is awkward, and from this point on you have a real climb on your hands. Once the overhang is reached an obvious escape is to move left into the deep crack (this is Candle Crack and is itself hard enough), but resist the temptation if you can, for the best climbing is only just starting.

    I remember on one particular blustery day climbing with a lightweight super strong Cliff Brown. The obvious rift in the scar at this point seemed to act as a wind tunnel and a constant jet stream made the top of the crags scream. Well this wasn't so bad but in addition, every so often a real blast would lift the smaller stones and anything else loose. We buried the sacs and gear below heavy rocks, and enthusiasm undaunted, set about the route. Cliff had reached the overhang and, fortunately, placed an excellent runner when we were hit by a particularly heavy gust. I've never seen anything quite like it before or since. Cliff catapulted horizontally out from the crag, carried by the force of the blast, until I managed to arrest his flight by hauling on the rope. The runner held, we were both OK and I note in my diary that The Candle was one of twelve routes we climbed despite the conditions.

    Assuming you stay in contact with the rock, the moves right and over the overhang are best described as powerful. The remainder of the route is contrasting in nature but remains top quality until you grasp a sharp-edged grike at the top.

    Evening Star and Priority are two routes chosen to match the pervading clean, airy and pleasant nature of the crag. The flakes are sharp, the angle steep and the climbing satisfying. Tony Greenbank, who first discovered the crag and did most to initiate development, was eager to seek my opinion on the grading. Appointed here are those we both think to be the most accurate. Elsewhere the grades are not so high. But see what you think.

NORTH YORK MOORS—PEAK SCAR

PEAK SCAR: Jordu, Pianississimo.
Map Ref: Se 527884.
Guidebooks: *Rock Climbing in Northern England* by Birkett & White. *Rock Climbs on the North York Moors* by The Cleveland Mountaineering Club/Cordee.
Attitude: Faces north.
Altitude: 850ft (260m).
Rock: Oolitic limestone; care must be taken with holds.
Access: A steep hill rises out of the little village of Hawnby to wind its way on to Boltby. When the road levels off to the horizontal, a little way beyond the point where the wood commences on the right, there is a tiny gate through the right fence and room to pull in and park. The crag lies in the woods below this. Through the gate a path drops steeply down into the wood and soon turns right to pass below the start of the cliff on the left. Initially the crag is overgrown and scruffy , but soon a clean wall stands out from the trees and vegetation. It is marked by a prominent chimney groove on its left side (5 minutes).
Observations: An unusual crag of great character with the wall described here, forming the major side of a wide ravine. The base and opposite side of the landslip feature are clothed in a variety of broadleaved trees providing shelter and adding charm to the location. The extensive crag grows in height to the right and is probably the most important in the North York Moors. The rock, although of the same geological type as Whitestone Cliff is much sounder here. However it should be treated with some respect, especially the large blocks that are occasionally encountered.

Chris Brueton in the corner of Jordu beneath the horizontal band of overhangs.

PEAK SCAR: Jordu, Pianississimo

JORDU: 75ft (23m), Very Difficult.
First Ascent: Terry Sullivan, Vic Tosh (*circa* 1961).
PIANISSISSIMO: 75ft (23m), Very Severe (4c).
First Ascent: Terry Sullivan, Vic Tosh (*circa* 1961).
Location: Peak Scar, North York Moors.

Jordu (Summary)

The left end of the first notable wall is marked by a distinct corner crack.

1. 75ft (23m). Climb the crack through the horizontal overlaps to a ledge on the left. Climb directly through the final horizontal overhang and continue up the crack to tree belays.

Pianississimo (Summary)

Start approximately 20ft right of the corner below a faint weakness leading to the first distinct horizontal break.

1. 75ft (23m), (4c). Climb the wall, trending leftwards, passing the first horizontal break to a detached block jammed beneath the horizontal overhanging barrier (The Battleship). Use this to reach above the barrier, pull up over it and continue to find a chimney weakness that leads easily to the top.

Jordu, Pianississimo (Description)

Autumn is probably the most attractive time to climb here. The vivid colours of the trees liven the mood of the drab grey limestone and the disappearing canopy gives a pleasant openness that is unfamiliar in the luxuriant summer months.

Despite the northerly aspect, the crag is well sheltered and nestling secretively in its little landslip ravine, the place has a unique atmosphere. The cliff is large and quite formidable, consisting as it does of a series of stepped out block overhangs all arranged in a linearly precise horizontal fashion. Not an altogether easy characteristic to explain however, is that it frequently appears more

Chris Brueton reaching over to gain the top of the Battleship on Pianississimo.

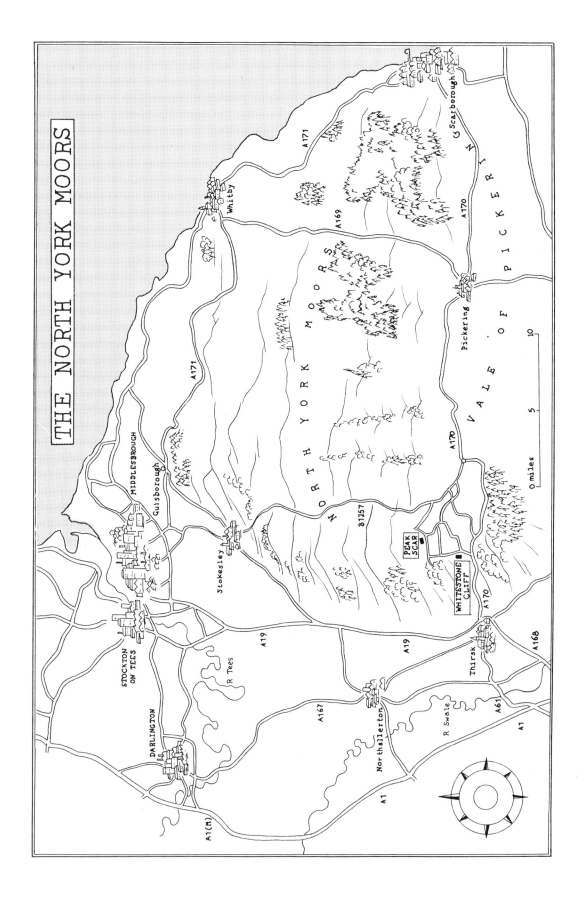

THE NORTH YORK MOORS

O belay point

Jordu

Pianississimo

friendly than sinister. Possibly this is because the overhangs tend to keep much of the wall dry and perhaps it is for this reason that it became one of my favourite crags in the North York Moors.

Jordu is quite an amazing little climb. It takes some extremely steep ground through the blocky bands and surmounts a number of overhangs, the last of which appears particularly awesome from below. But the holds are remarkably good, the crack of suitable width to make solid hand jams, and the frequent horizontal bands make for regular footholds. If it is actually raining, or if misty/moisty conditions prevail, a little restraint should be exercised at the top, for once the largest overhang is passed the roof-like rain protection disappears which can leave the rock muddy or greasy.

Pianississimo is appropriately named. A bold route requiring a very gentle touch. Even the initial wall is demanding and the small pocket holds are best assessed from a distance prior to starting. It is only after technical and finger strenuous moves that a runner can be found in the distinct horizontal break. Most will hang about to place it.

Moving up to the overhanging barrier is not so difficult, but on reaching it, one could be excused a little trepidation. Firstly it is more substantial than it looks from a distance, and secondly, even more importantly, the nature of the rock may give rise to some concern.

The holds you launch off from (jammed blocks wedged in the crack separating the overhanging band from the rest of the cliff), do nothing to inspire confidence. And when you grasp the top of the horizontal break, The Battleship, it does your already pounding heart no good at all to realise that it is apparently detached from the rest of the cliff. Softly, softly does it.

Jordu and Pianississimo on Peak Scar.

NORTH YORK MOORS—WHITESTONE CLIFF

WHITESTONE CLIFF: Nightwatch.
Map Ref: SE 507836.
Guidebooks: *Rock Climbing in Northern England* by Birkett & White. *Rock Climbs on the North York Moors* by The Cleveland Mountaineering Club/Cordee.
Attitude: Faces west.
Altitude: 1000ft (300m).
Rock: An usual oolitic limestone, generally quite weak in nature—care should be taken at all times.
Access: The A170 from Thirsk winds up Sutton Bank to a large car park and visitor centre at the top. Follow the path north from here—The Cleveland Way—along the top of the edge. After a mile or so the bushes and scrub clears and an unbroken view across the plains below (and back over Gormire Lake) can be had. The edge of the cliff has been reached. The long face stretches northwards from here but the point of access lies down a steep gully just below. The top of the gully is steep grass but this soon wears out and becomes polished clay. In the dry it is tricky enough, but if at all wet, the descent becomes precarious and it may be advisable to fix up a rope. There is a small tree as the grass disappears but anything more substantial can only be found some way back. The climb lies on the distinct wall around the prominent prow to the right—looking out— (15 minutes).

Observations: This is a substantial cliff, the largest in the North York Moors, but for much of its length the rock is fundamentally unsound. The climb described is the safest here, but even so, one should be prepared for holds breaking off without warning. The rock is absolutely unique (thankfully) and resembles a dolly mixture of limestone/sandstone rubble stuck together with some weak sandy cement. Despite everything it occupies a fine position and gives climbing of great character.

Harvesting the bilberries on Whitestone Cliff.

WHITESTONE CLIFF: Nightwatch

NIGHTWATCH: 110ft (34m), Hard Severe (4a).
First Ascent: Terry Sullivan (*circa* 1960s).
Location: Whitestone Cliff, North York Moors.

Nightwatch (Summary)

The climb couldn't be more obvious—the distinct corner crack up the right hand end of a long straight wall.

1. 110ft (34m), (4a). Climb the corner crack using the frequent, if not obvious from below, horizontal breaks. The difficulties are sustained to the top. A belay tree will be found well back from the top.

Nightwatch (Description)

Back in my student days in the north-east, my climbing mate Rick Graham, knowingly commented that if you could make a free descent of Whitestone Cliff then you could climb any line on the crag. Perhaps so, perhaps not, but in the wet the descent does provide excellent training for descending ice couloirs—without an ice axe. Thinking about it crampons would probably be ideal. But enough of this let us move on to the selected climb.

The steep, overhanging in places, corner crack, forms an imposing and impressive line. It is defined on its right by a prow of rock which steps out in a series of overhangs as it soars up the crag and on the right by a plumb vertical wall. Therefore, in true classic tradition, Nightwatch is the easiest way to breach the cliff's defences.

The rock on this climb is the best on the cliff, and the deep rift, in addition to the dark security to be achieved by full body immersion, offers good pockets and enough runners to just justify the ascent at the grade appendaged. In fact the route is not as formidable as initial appearances would suggest, although the first-time visitor to the cliff could be forgiven for thinking the route to be somewhat undergraded and this is a point worth bearing in mind.

John Lockley, having passed the overhangs on Nightwatch, continues up the corner; Gormire Lake can be seen below.

Nightwatch on Whitestone Crag.

Take care should you venture elsewhere on the cliff for the rock is most peculiar. The wall bounding Nightwatch is quite white, as one would expect from the name of the cliff, but elsewhere the crag has an unmistakeably orange tinge, heightened most beautifully as the sun sets. In these areas the whole structure of the cliff is suspect and gives the impression that it is gradually decomposing. The composition resembles a mix of limestone and sandstone rubble, randomly speckled with large egg-shaped boulders, all held together with a very weak sandy cement. Many of the holds have the strength of hollow sugar and although the actual lines look inviting, prudence is most definitely the wisest form of valour.

You get used to the sudden whoosh and rattle as the gliders scrape over the top and once you make a start up the vertical crack you will soon settle to the task at hand. The climbing through the overhanging bits above can't really fail to bemuse. It's so different to how you expect it to be, and it involves everything from chimneying and wall climbing through to roof climbing and back again to slab climbing a little way below the top. The variety of holds and techniques you have to apply are equally diverse and the standard is sustained throughout.

Nightwatch is a remarkably fruitful climb, enhanced further because it is not at all what it first seems. However, although this probably goes without saying, make an effort to utilise each and every good runner placement you find. The tree belay is miles back and it's worth warning the second man before you set off that you may be some little time finding and fixing it before you return to the edge to protect and encourage—time that can be somewhat extended on a sunny summer's day at the height of the bilberry season. Bon appetit, enjoy the view.

CUMBRIA—LAZONBY

LAZONBY: Merry Monk.
Map Ref: NY 527423.
Guidebooks: *Rock Climbing in Northern England* by Birkett & White. *North of England* by S. G. Wilson and R. J. Kenyon.
Attitude: Faces north east.
Altitude: 250ft (75m).
Rock: Sandstone, generally good but care should be taken.
Access: From the A6 Penrith-to-Carlisle road, turn off at Plumpton for the village of Lazonby. Pass under the railway bridge in the village then take a narrow road leading off to the left. A couple of miles down this road, unfenced open land opens out on the right and shortly after this, over the brow of the hill, a track can be spotted—a pile of boulders a little way down marks its path. There is ample parking here. Follow the track which leads to a bridge over the railway line. After closing the gate, turn right and follow a path past a circular planting of conifers and continue along the path (high brackens) until a stone wall and large fir trees mark the top of the crag. Continue until a broad incline leads down to the upstream side of Wirewalk Buttress by the side of the River Eden (15 minutes). There is no public right of way and to maintain the present free access please ensure you park sensibly and check all gates are shut and no litter is left.

Observations: The buttress rises directly out of the River Eden and offers interesting climbing in a fine environment. Climbing can be had here most of the year round and the rock dries reasonably quickly. The rock is soft red sandstone, generally good, but care should be exercised.

O belay point

Above: **Merry Monk on Lazonby.**

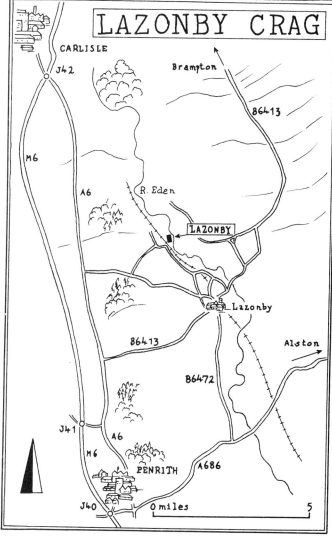

LAZONBY: Merry Monk

MERRY MONK: 110ft (33m), Hard Very Severe (5a).
First Ascent: Alan Beatty, John Simpson, John Workman (*circa* 1970).
Location: Wirewalk Buttress, Lazonby, Cumbria.

Merry Monk (Summary)

A path with a wire handrail leads round the base of the cliff just above the water. The first wide corner groove cannot be missed and marks the line of this climb.

1. 85ft (26m), (5a). Follow the corner until it becomes overhung (possible stance before this). Move up and out to the right in an exposed position. Continue to a ledge where it may be best to belay to avoid rope drag.

2. 25ft (7m), (4a). Climb the steep short wall to pull up and out to the right. Belay a little way beyond the edge.

Merry Monk (Description)

The crag was initially discovered and developed by the Penrith lads and it wasn't for some time that details of their secret crag leaked to the outside world. It surely proved a difficult secret to keep, for to discover a crag of this magnitude as late as the end of the sixties must have been tremendously exciting. The climbing is steep and demanding and the line described here the most natural of all the climbs on the Eden Valley sandstone.

The red-black sandstone proves unusual and features frequent ripple bands of wafer-thin flakes. These provide hand and footholds but cannot be absolutely relied upon not to snap off. It is basically a question of common sense. The sandstone used wisely with at least two other points of contact, will present few problems, for if one hold breaks the other two will maintain your essential contact with the rock.

The setting above the Eden is refined and gentle, and the character of the area quite different to what most would expect to find in the new county of Cumbria. The area is part of the old Cumberland and it feels much closer to Scotland in atmosphere and architecture than the nearby Wordsworth's

Luke Steer begins Merry Monk from the wire walkway, just above the river.

akeland. The mighty pines standing roudly at the top of the crag further ompound this impression.

If the river is exceptionally high, it is ossible though unlikely, you will get your et wet, for if you should by chance lose ontact with the wirewalk (the wire handrail s not above suspicion), then your chances of urvival would depend on your swimming rowess for rapids lie below.

The name of the climb is jolly enough but lakes one curious as to why it was chosen, or this was one of the earliest routes on a ewly-found climbing ground. You could educe that the barrel-shaped buttress fired houghts of a notable local brew of tradition- l beer from the wood. Or perhaps the Junnery Walks on the immediate opposite ide of the river had something to do with it. 'hatting with Alan Beatty, one of the limbers to make the first ascent of this oute and one responsible for much of the arly development, it seems that this latter peculation would not be wide of the mark. Ie revealed the source of the name came om a cave they discovered on a nearby uttress which leads to a balcony with a fine iew across the river. A monk's cell—a room ith a view!

The climb provides much of interest. A old route following the most obvious eature on the crag providing absorbing limbing and quite sensational exposure. Iowever it must be admitted there was an chilles Heel to the route when I climbed it: reat dollops of white lime covered most of he route for some bird had chosen it as a esting site. The quantity was quite remark- ble and one could be forgiven for thinking was the last nesting place of the Great uk. A kestrel or owl is the more likely ulprit however.

Bird lime apart, the line and the climbing appealing enough, providing an absorb- g exercise in bridging until one is stopped y the overhanging cap above the groove. ome may wish to belay below this point, nd although the stance is poor, there are ood belays to be had. The climbing at the op of the groove rapidly becomes very steep nd the moves out right are extremely xposed. Although this is the most difficult ection of the route it is relatively short and weet. Above, whilst the position remains otably open, with a straight drop into the iver below, the technical difficulties are much more reasonable. Anyhow there isn't uch further to go before you too can enjoy he view.

Luke Steer wide-bridging up the groove of Merry Monk; the white substance isn't ice!

95

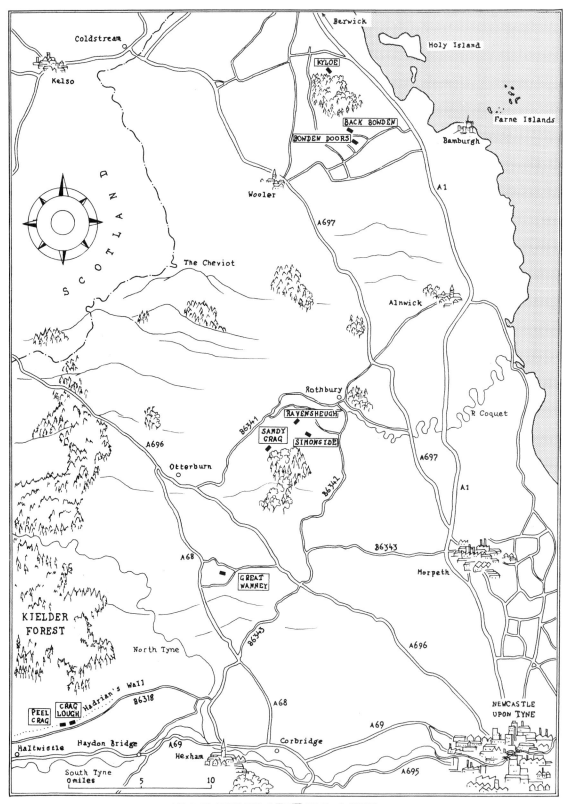

NORTHUMBERLAND

NORTHUMBERLAND—BACK BOWDEN DOORS

BACK BOWDEN DOORS: The Tube, The Arches.
Map Ref: NU 065336.
Guidebooks: *Rock Climbing in Northern England* by Birkett & White. *Northumberland* by Northumberland Mountaineering Club.
Attitude: Faces south west.
Altitude: 560ft (170m).
Rock: Sandstone.
Access: Leave the A1 at Belford and from the village follow the B6349 towards Wooler. Where the road forks go right, until roughly at the crest of the hill, there is a gate on the right (approximately 3 miles from Belford). There is restricted parking on the verge here. Go through the gate and along the track to another gate. After this a path soon drops down into a little valley to a small bridge and gate over a stream. Just above this is a two-tiered buttress. The clean soaring prow that marks the end of The Tube Wall lies a few hundred yards further along and the main section of crag starts from here (8 minutes).
Observations: Lying in a sheltered valley, with half the crag further protected by a pine forest, this is a delightful place to climb. It is noted for its grossly overhanging nature and the roof-like overhangs that guard the mid section of the crag. The local name for this crag is Colour Heugh and there is no right of access. Fortunately access has not been a problem in the past, however, recent behaviour has placed the situation under review. To maintain the free access situation please do not bivouac (hoff) below the rooves, light fires, build or damage walls or leave litter. Additionally considerable damage has been caused by climbers running their top ropes over the sandstone edges. Because of the geologically soft nature of the rock (although the rock is excellent to climb upon) this scours out deep runnels—starting an irreversible process of erosion. It is essential that this ceases; if climbers must top rope then the live ropes are to be extended by long slings over the edges of the crag in such a manner as to prevent wear to the rock.

John Earl climbing The Tube on Back Bowden Doors.

○ belay point

The Tube

BACK BOWDEN DOORS: The Tube

THE TUBE: 50ft (15m), E4 (5c).
First Ascent: Bob Hutchinson, John Earl
(*circa* 1978).
Location: Tube Wall, Back Bowden Doors,
Northumberland.

The Tube (Summary)

Left of the soaring prow a diagonal crack
cleaves the wall. Start up this.

1. 50ft (15m), (5c). Climb the crack
leftwards to a ledge. Move right up the
scoop to gain a hand traverse line below the
tube. Traverse right for 20ft until it is
possible to pull through the tube to the top.

The Tube (Description)

Back Bowden Doors is an evocative climbing ground requiring in the main strong
arms and not a little ability. Whilst most
looking for hard problems will initially try
their hand on the climbs that take the
remarkable horizontal roof to the left of The
Tube Wall, those intent on doing a full-
blooded route will return to take on the
challenge of The Tube. Although blatantly
bold, this is also an intricate and technical
line requiring good climbing craft to rope
protect the lower section.

To most, the technical crux will be
moving up the rightward trending scoop
above the ledge. The section above this,
however, seeking out a weakness to pull over
the cylindrical overhang, is relentlessly strenuous. Protection can be placed regularly,
but with friction on the vertical and smooth
wall offering only minimal backup support

for pumping arms, most will want to pres
on as quickly as possible.

When the point to move over the tube i
finally located, a high runner offers excellen
security, though having the strength and
composure to place it may not be ar
automatic process. Then enough holds wil
be found to escape the strenuosity and wha
a feeling of elation, even if the knees and
stomach do assist the transfer from vertica
to horizontal, to finally surf through the
tube.

Looking along the sandstone edge of
Back Bowden Doors to the conifer
plantation.

BACK BOWDEN DOORS: The Arches

THE ARCHES: 50ft (15m), Hard Very Severe (5a).
First Ascent: Rodney Wilson (1965).
Location: Left-hand section of Back Bowden Doors, Northumberland.

The Arches (Summary)

This climb can be located some way beyond the obvious roof section (found where the crag enters the forest) towards the left end of the crag. Start up the noticeably black rock of the left end of the sandwiched slab.

1. 50ft (25m), (5a). Step up onto the slab and make an ascending traverse rightwards with overhangs above and space below. Keep traversing until the slab ends in a steep groove and take this and the flutings above to the top.

The Arches (Description)

This is a remarkable route taking a natural hanging slab through some considerably overhanging ground. Commencing just right of the most cavernous section of the crag, with its black rock often dappled by a sun already filtered by the conifers, the scene is set for an atmospheric climb. Step boldly onto the slab and don't worry about the blackness of the rock for the sandstone is perfectly sound.

This is a route of surprising length and despite the initial cave-like start, progress becomes remarkably exposed in a very few feet. It is intimidating too, so it is essential to keep calm as the overhangs above oppress the spirit and the space below plucks at your feet. With the body doubled by the physical constraints of the sandwich, often you cannot see any holds in the roof or a specific direction in which the slab will best unfold itself. But holds enough are there, the grade is fair, and even at the end when a vertical bottomless groove presents itself, the observant will be amply rewarded.

Below left: **Ian Kyle on the sandwiched slab of The Arches.**

Below right: **Ian Kyle gaining the end of the ramp.**

Above: **The Arches on Back Bowden Doors.**

Left: **John Earl powering out of The Tube after the hand traverse.**

NORTHUMBERLAND—BOWDEN DOORS

BOWDEN DOORS: **Main Wall, Lorraine, Poseidon Adventure.**

Map Ref: NU 070325.

Guidebooks: *Rock Climbing in Northern England* by Birkett & White. *Northumberland* by Northumberland Mountaineering Club.

Attitude: Faces south west.

Altitude: 560ft (170m).

Rock: Sandstone.

Access: Leave the A1 at Belford and from the village follow the B6349 towards Wooler. Where the road forks keep left until, at the highest point, the end of the crag can just be seen on the right. This is about three miles from Belford and the verge is just wide enough to take cars sensibly parked (do not block the field entrances). The gate on the right provides access to the southern end (Main Wall section) of the crag (2 minutes). Lorraine and Poseidon Adventure are situated towards the far, northern, end of the crag. The crags lie in the grounds of North Lytham Farm who allow free access at the time of writing. Shut the gate after you, leave no litter and take care not to damage the stone walls that run up to the crag.

Observations: A major sandstone edge. Never rising above 40ft in height but offering a huge number of high quality routes of tremendous character, the crag culminates in the unique Wave Buttress near its north end. Fine weather can often be enjoyed here when the rest of the county is wet. A climbing ground very much in the modern idiom where most of the routes are inevitably strenuous and of a highly technical nature.

O belay point

Main Wall: John Earl starting up the first clean wall on the crag.

BOWDEN DOORS: Main Wall

MAIN WALL: 45ft (14m), Hard Very Severe (5b).
First Ascent: Malcom Rowe (*circa* 1969).
Location: Main Wall area, southern end Bowden Doors, Northumberland.

Main Wall (Summary)

Takes a central line up the first distinct wall—Main Wall. Start beneath a shallow flake corner.

1. 45ft (14m), (5b). Climb the vague corner to move out right. Climb the wall until it is easier to traverse left to gain the distinct finishing crack running up the centre of the headwall.

Main Wall (Description)

This, the first obvious line when approaching from the road, gives excellent climbing up the plumb vertical wall. All the holds are positive and it serves as an excellent introduction to the hard climbing to be found here.

One of the higher climbs to be found on this edge means that most people will care to rope up and lead rather than solo this enjoyable route of sustained difficulty. John Earle, however, soloed it for my cameras, adding harder variations and traverses to keep moving and warm as I changed position. OK for the expert who knows the crag and the area like his back yard, but for the first-timer to the cliff the standard line should prove interesting enough.

My first visit to the crag, on a rather cold and blustery day and when the cracks all weeped a little green, saw me on Main Wall. It looked easy; it was strenuous. It looked insignificantly short; it felt remarkably sustained. On top, buffeted by a strong wind, finger tips stinging from attrition and cold, the potential of this remarkable edge began to dawn on me. This initial wall is merely vertical, the rest of the three quarters of a mile of sandstone that makes up Bowden Doors is mainly overhanging.

Looking across the rolling upland of Northumberland to the far northern end of Bowden Doors.

102

BOWDEN DOORS: Lorraine

LORRAINE: 35ft (11m), Very Severe (5a).
First Ascent: Malcom Rowe (1968).
Location: Towards the north end of Bowden Doors, Northumberland.

Lorraine (Summary)

The climb is reached by walking north along the edge until a little way after crossing the second wall that abuts the crag (the one that continues in the same line above the crag), an overhanging wall offers an unmistakeable layback flake.

1. 35ft (11m), (5a). Climb the flake to make a high reach to gain the higher horizontal break. Hand traverse left until a standing position can be gained in the break. Move up onto the delicate friction slab to make a bold finish.

Lorraine (Description)

A climb of great character and contrast which packs a mighty lot into its short length and comparatively, for the edge, lowly grade. The flake leads powerfully up the overhanging wall demanding cool control despite its arm-wrenching nature. Near the top a reach gains the horizontal break. Most will move left as rapidly as possible to force up into a standing position in the break and take the pressure off the arms.

From the ridiculous to the sublime, the next moves up the blank wall which separates you from the finish, require a fine degree of balance and faith in the frictional qualitites of Northumberland sandstone. Protection in the break lessens the feeling of seriousness, although the brave may spurn it, but even so, a level of mental energy is required to commence the sequence.

Not a route to experiment with. Total commitment and a corresponding level of arm strength and fitness are required for success. Very Severe? The experts insist this is correct, and who am I to disagree; the traditional grade you understand.

Andy Birtwistle at the end of the hand traverse on Lorraine; from here you pull up and stand in the break.

BOWDEN DOORS: Poseidon Adventure

POSEIDON ADVENTURE: 33ft (10m), E4 (6a).
First Ascent: Steve Blake (*circa* 1978).
Location: Wave Wall, north end of Bowden Doors, Northumberland.

Poseidon Adventure (Summary)

A long frozen wave crests and overhangs a smooth vertical wall near the northern-most extremity of the crag. This is Wave Wall and the route starts approximately mid way along the first section of wall.

1. 33ft (10m), (6a). Follow the weakness to the blank section below the brake. A move pinching a chicken head enables a long reach to be made to the break below the wave. Traverse right until an undercut in the wave above, enables one to stand in the break. Reach over the top of the wave (it is hollow at this point), and move left to make a final spectacular pull to surmount the wave.

Poseidon Adventure (Description)

Wave Wall is one of the most memorably aesthetic features of all the northern England outcrops. The petrified wave, which would not appear out of place running along the beach of nearby Holy Island, crowns a smooth, steep, almost featureless wall. In the afternoon sun the wave shines gold above the lighter wall below; a dramatic effect heightened further when the brackens have died back red.

Poseidon Adventure follows the most obvious tangible weakness up the bottom wall to gain and climb the wave. It is a spectacular and powerful route which offers no protection for the roped—it is therefore usual to tackle it solo. All this adds up to a very exacting climb, a modern test piece where it is essential for the would-be ascensionist to appreciate the possible consequences of a fall.

Initially the wall lies back just off the vertical, and a thin, upside down layback crack, leads to the short vertical wall barring access to the break below the wave. If you are tall, achieving this may prove to be the crux of the route, but if you are short the next moves, pinching a chicken head with the right hand may prove the most difficult.

The short must first move high on the ruggosity, pulling with the right hand, but then to reach the break some way above, you must turn the hold to undercut in order to obtain the necessary height to gain the break. The thought of an uncontrolled fall from this point, with feet and hands screaming from the rock involuntarily, to spiral disasterously to the hard ground below is one that proves too much for many. The softer alternative, of looking and making a controlled jump, becomes surprisingly attractive.

Should you make the moves, keep your bottle, then it is still necessary to maintain tight control. Safe jumping from the break is out of the question and there is still a way to go before a final spectacular swing cuts the feet loose and pulls the body up and over the golden wave.

Bob Smith, who has recently pioneered some of the hardest climbs in the area, made light work of the route twice in succession in order that I should get some reasonable shots. As he hung nonchalantly on the undercut below the wave, shaking out and, on my request waiting for the next burst of fleeting sunshine, one could have been forgiven for forgetting the strenuous and perilous nature of his position. However, when the sun weakly returned and he powered from the undercut to cut loose and crest the wave, the full impact of this masterpiece was again vividly apparent.

Bob Smith on the hand break beneath the wave on Poseidon Adventure.

NORTHUMBERLAND—CRAG LOUGH

CRAG LOUGH: Main Wall.
Map Ref: NY 765679.
Guidebooks: *Rock Climbing in Northern England* by Birkett & White. *Northumberland* by Northumberland Mountaineering Club.
Attitude: Faces north west.
Altitude: 850ft (260m).
Rock: Whin Sill.
Access: Hadrian's Wall runs along the crest of Crag Lough and access is along this. Turn off the B6318 Military Road northwards at the Once Brewed junction to park in the Steel Rigg car park (free). From the car park can be seen Peel Crag and beyond this, above the little lake (the lough), lies Crag Lough. Take the path to the Roman Wall and proceed along over the top of Peel Crags until the end of the crag is reached. The climb lies on the largest buttress, named Central Buttress, to the left end of the crag (15 minutes).
Descent: Walk around right to the end of the crags or scramble down a steep gully just right of the top of the Central Buttress. The gully head has an obvious wooden fence around it to safeguard tourists.
Observations: This is one of the largest crags in the area consisting of a number of individual buttresses separated by steep broken and vegetated rocks. The Central Buttress is the largest of these and reaches a height of 100ft (33m). It is a wild location, full of atmosphere, and only gets the sunshine late in the day. The rock is the black, hard Whin Sill—a compact quartz dolerite—and this makes the climbing quite different to anything else experienced in Northumberland; indeed different to anything else in England.

O belay point

Main Wall

Main Wall on Crag Lough.

CRAG LOUGH: Main Wall

MAIN WALL: 100ft (33m), Severe.
First Ascent: Basil Butcher, Keith Gregory
(*circa* 1940).
Location: Central Buttress, Crag Lough,
Northumberland.

Main Wall (Summary)

The Central Buttress is the last major
buttress of rock on Crag Lough and is
distinctively the highest. The climb takes
the face of the main pillar and starts from
the lowest point of the rocks.

    1. 100ft (33m). Climb easily to a sticking-
out block. From a standing position on this,
move up left to gain a horizontal break for
the hands (crux). Move up and right to a
ledge on the edge. Follow the groove above,
which leads to an absorbing chimney, which
may be found harder than the technical
crux. The chimney leads to a ledge a little
way below the top. There are belays here
and it may be preferable to take them.
Above, a few feet of easy rocks lead to the
top of the buttress and Hadrian's Wall.

Main Wall (Description)

Whilst the actual border line dividing north
and south, Scotland and England, may have
shifted some way further north, spiritually
Hadrian's Wall still separates the softer
south from the uncontrollably wild lands of
the north. Plunging away proudly below the
Wall, an integral part of its defences, Crag
Lough is atmospherically very much a
frontier outpost; a unique climbing ground
with a lot to offer both the romantic and the
rock climber.

    The black rock is hard, compact and
takes on a vertical columnar, pillar-like
structure. Geologically it resulted when
molten magma, forced upwards, became
trapped to form a subterranean lake. This in

Looking from the north to Main Wall, note Hadrian's Wall runs along the crest of this natural defence.

turn cooled in such a manner as to form separately jointed columns of rock. The subsequent strata, resulting from the erosion of the softer upper rocks, resembles that of other notable climbing cliffs such as the Kilt Rock on the east coast of the Isle of Skye or that of the distinct Devil's Tower in Wyoming.

Bearing this in mind, it is easier to understand the climbing characteristics of the crag. It is necessary to be able to fully utilise the straight vertical parallel sided cracks, which vary in width from thin finger-size to back-and-footing chimneys, and to make the most of the flat ledges. These features are respectively the sides and tops of the columns. Keith Gregory writing about the pioneering years of the 1940s had the following observations to make regarding the climbing of the Crag Lough Whin Sill:

'This is not the rock where holds snap off, but when B. A. B. was doing a new lead, a huge monolith moved outwards with extreme slowness and he was only able to get clear as it leant over and crashed down. Holds are generally wide apart and square, no jug handles. Since the rock is smooth and hard, rubbers and the liberal use of pressure holds is the easiest way of getting up.[1]'

Main Wall is a climb right at the top of its grade. In fact a first visitor to the crag may feel that the standard is somewhat higher than the Severe appendage given here. However, with some understanding of the nature of the crag and the type of climbing best employed, the grade is justifiable. Because the rock is so compact, between the faults, and because its make-up is essentially vertical, intermediate footholds are few and far between. In general it is therefore necessary to maximise the cracks and to move quickly and confidently on the steep ground between the breaks. Having said this, Main Wall, which is the most striking and continuous line to be found on Crag Lough, offers climbing with variety sufficient to balance its intensity.

Initial climbing from the foot of the front face leads to a ledge with a rattly sticking out block. From here things liven up considerably and moves up left are at the same time strenuous and precarious until a horizontal break for the hands can be reached. Nut protection is excellent. After a ledge on

1. 1946 *Journal of the Fell & Rock Climbing Club*—'Climbing in Northumberland' by H. K. Gregory.

Fiona Mirlees tackling the crux of the lower wall of Main Wall.

the right edge of the pillar provides a useful rest the nature of the climbing changes. The transition from bold face climbing to the comfortable recessed groove above may not prove unwelcome.

This groove, however, soon terminates in a deep, smooth, vertical-sided chimney. Paradoxically chimneys can often prove both precarious, in that you feel a relaxation of muscle and effort will see you shooting down and out of the bottom at a considerable rate of knots, and impossibly restrictive, as you fight and scrabble to inch your

way upwards from your strenuously jammed position. This one proves to be no exception. On the contrary it is really rather a champion of chimneys!

Crag Lough was traditionally one of the most popular of Northumbrian crags. Whilst its devotees undoubtedly remain faithful, the more northerly sandstone crags now see the main volume of traffic. If you are lucky, this means that, even on a perfect midsummer's day, only the swans gliding gracefully on the dark lough below may be there to keep you company.

GREAT WANNEY: Idiot's Delight, Great Wall, Northumberland Wall.
Map Ref: NY 935835.
Guidebooks: *Rock Climbing in Northern England* by Birkett & White. *Northumberland* by Northumberland Mountaineering Club.
Attitude: Faces north west.
Altitude: 1, 000ft (320m).
Rock: Sandstone.
Access: One of the most southerly of the Northumbrian sandstone crags, it is reached by turning off the A696 Newcastle to Otterburn road at Knowesgate. After a few miles the road forks and it is best to turn right (although the left fork leads to Sweethope Lough from where a boggy approach leads up to the top of the crag), until just beyond the bottom of a large dip in the road double gates on the left close the entrance to the Forestry Commission wood. There is ample parking here, but be sure not to block the access. Follow the track beyond the gates until it veers off to the right. At this point a break is followed directly ahead and where this emerges from the wood the crag can be seen more or less straight ahead. A path leads directly to the rocks (20 minutes). Although there is no public right of way there do not appear to be any access problems at the time of writing.

Observations: A justifiably popular crag offering good climbs of all grades. The rock is excellent but its altitude and exposed nature can make it rather a cold venue, additionally it does seem to rain here when many other locations, albeit situated somewhat further north, remain dry.

b&w 48
Idiot's Delight, Great Wall and Northumberland Wall on Great Wanney.

○ belay point

GREAT WANNEY: Idiot's Delight, Great Wall, Northumberland Wall

IDIOT'S DELIGHT: 40ft (12m), Hard Severe (4a).
First Ascent: (Probably) A. P. Rossiter (*circa* late 1930s).
GREAT WALL: 50ft (15m), Hard Very Severe (5b).
First Ascent: Mick Foggan, Hugh Banner 1972).
NORTHUMBERLAND WALL: 50ft (15m), E2 (5b).
First Ascent: Bob Hutchinson, John Earl *circa* 1976).
Location: Great Wanney, Northumberland.

Idiot's Delight (Summary)

The climb lies near the left (east) end of the crag a few yards right of where the boundry wall and little swing gate join the crag. Start to the right of the rib.

1. 40ft (12m), (4a). Climb the scoop and groove to a cave. Move out left until a pull up onto the slab enables a delicate step to be made up the rib. Finish directly.

Great Wall (Summary)

The wall on the right is started via the short chimney.

1. 50ft (15m), (5b). Take the chimney to the niche and climb the thin crack until a horizontal break allows one to traverse right. From the end of the traverse pull steeply up into a shallow corner and move up this to the ledge on the right shoulder. It is possible to belay, but if one continues, care should be taken to prevent rope drag. The short but impending groove provides a fitting finale and the technical crux.

Northumberland Wall (Summary)

Starts in a bay a little way over to the right. The line begins up the obvious groove in the right wall.

1. 50ft (15m), (5b). Take the groove and continue up the steep crack in the upper wall. Below the top a horizontal break is reached and this is used to step right before pulling directly over to finish a very fine climb. Regular nut placements make this an adequately protected route.

Idiot's Delight. Above the traverse from the cave and the delicate scoop, Andy Birtwistle gains the final rib.

Great Wanney can be approached from below or over the back.

Idiot's Delight, Great Wall and Northumberland Wall (Description)

The location of the Great Wanney crags, scarcely more than twenty miles from Newcastle, ensured their popularity from the turn of the century onwards. The rocks, despite their rather taciturn and scraggy appearance offer some excellent climbs. The crag is best described as being made up of a number of blocky buttresses and recesses, the walls of which tend to be vertical or overhanging. But the sandstone holds are good and there are climbs covering the whole spectrum of difficulty. The three routes selected here represent the best of their respective grades. Taken individually, they would rank as distinguished climbs anywhere.

Idiot's Delight used to be known as Raven Nest climb. However, the rapidly increasing popularity of the crags saw the resident raven vacating the cave to climbers who are equally grateful of its security and comfort. It is a place to pause, to gather both strength and courage before the sensational and strenuous traverse left. Hence the present name?

It is a climb full of surprises, one in which the climbing interest far outweighs its meagre lineage. For this book I photographed a very young Andrew Earl, seconding Andy Birtwistle. His able performance certainly showed his climbing pedigree, Son of John Earl—one of Northumbria's and Lakeland's leading pioneers—he shot up the bottom scoop and groove and, barely pausing for breath hand traversed left. Only, due to his lack of physical height his hands were on the normal line of footholds. At the end of

the traverse, feet in space, he made som wild-looking pulls to shoot rapidly back u to the normal level of ascent. Apparently o an even earlier occasion, presumably whe a few vital inches shorter, on leaving th cave he laybacked on an upside down flak with his feet at the normal hand level. A the irrepressibility of youth.

Great Wall is aptly named and involve some solid climbing up this smooth conca face. It links the bottom crack with an ex out right, over what looks to be, from belov extremely hard ground. There is a dire finish at a considerably increased standar of difficulty, but the moves to the rig follow a natural horizontal break, one whic offers excellent jams. In turn these enable crescent-shaped flake to be reached in rearing groove. It is now only a little furth to gain the castellated break on the rig shoulder of the wall.

A vulgarly leaning groove now separates you from the top. This is the technical crux and requires a move back left to overview the steep wall below before you finally crack the problem; a satisfying route, never exactly desperate, but sustained and with much interest. Finding a belay is another problem, but there is a block some way back that takes an indifferent nut and a contrived friend placement. Best make doubly sure that what you get is safe, for it is not uncommon for a second, pushing the grade, to make a slip or two.

Northumberland Wall is appropriately named and a tremendous climb. Unrelentingly steep, the difficulties are remarkably sustained from top to bottom. Cold fingers will make a great deal of difference as the initial groove soon bulges to offer up a finger technical crack which rises up the hanging headwall of the pinnacle-like buttress to terminate short of the top. Despite the steepness it is quite feasible to stop and place runners in the crack and, adding to the enjoyment of the route the runner placements that come up are good. Then, just when the crack dies, and strength begins to ebb, a neat sequence of handholds enable moves right, placing you in a good position to make the reach for the top. A quick arm heave and over you go, an exacting and exciting route right to the last.

John Earl, who accompanied the late Bob Hutchinson on the first ascent, climbed the route again to enable me to get some shots. In doing so he explained a mystery that had been puzzling me for some time. High in the crack there is a wedge of concrete blocking up what would be quite a sizeable hold. It certainly maintains the standard of the climbing and, because it consists of sand and pebbles from the foot of the route mixed with cement, many involved with the intricacies of the climbing at this point will fail to observe that it isn't actually a natural part of the crag.

However, John explained that after they had made the ascent someone else came along and hammered a block out of the crack to create a large artificial hold. The guilty party having lowered the standard of the climb to his own abilities subsequently climbed the route using this man-made hold. Bob, who was to be later tragically killed in the Lake District prospecting a new route, thought this act to be unjustified and filled in the offending hold with his environmentally sensitive concrete. So the route now stands to be enjoyed in its original form—a very fine climb created and recreated by one of Northumberland's great rock climbing pioneers.

Andy Moss entering the niche of Great Wall.

John Earl belaying Andy Birtwistle on Northumberland Wall, the final few feet.

NORTHUMBERLAND—KYLOE CRAG

KYLOE CRAG: Flake Crack, Tacitation.
Map Ref: NU 040395.
Guidebooks: *Rock Climbing in Northern England* by Birkett & White. *Northumberland* by Northumberland Mountaineering Club.
Attitude: Faces south west.
Altitude: 330ft (100m).
Rock: Sandstone.
Access: From the A1 take the Fenwick junction to gain the B6353. Continue along this through West Kyloe until a road junction enables a left turn to be made into the road that eventually leads along the edge of Kyloe Wood. Before the wood is reached, farm buildings are passed on the left and after these there is a wide gate also on the left (there is a further building between this point and the wood). The verge provides adequate parking and after the gate a track leads through the fields. The track is a public right of way which leads over the top of the crag. However, just before the crags are reached, a right fork is taken and a path leads along under the buttresses. Occasionally there is an electric fence crossing the track. Rather than straddle over this with possible disastrous consequences an insulated hook will be found on one side and this lifts up to allow free passage (10 minutes).

Observations: An attractive crag consisting of a number of separate buttresses that look across to the edge of Kyloe Wood. There is a fair selection of routes of all grades and the sheltered sunny position makes it a good venue. This northerly area of Northumberland (and the Bowden Doors crags) lies in the rain-shadow of the Cheviot Hills and it is quite often dry here when raining elsewhere. This and the fact it is placed equidistantly between Newcastle and Edinburgh ensure its popularity. The routes are situated on 'C' Buttress which lies near the right end of the crag; a sizeable gully-like recess is bounded on its right by a clean tall wall.

O belay point

b&w 50
One climber finishes Flake Crack while another starts Tacitation.

FLAKE CRACK: 35ft (11m), Severe (4a).
First Ascent: Eric Clark, G. Lewis, Basil Butcher (*circa* 1950s).
TACITATION: 30ft (9m), Hard Very Severe (5b).
First Ascent: Nev Hannaby (*circa* 1950s).
Location: 'C' Buttress, Kyloe Crag, Northumberland.

Flake Crack (Summary)

Start at the flake crack placed approximately in the centre of the wall.

1. 35ft (11m). The flake crack is followed with interest until it terminates a little way below the top. Finish directly up the wall.

Tacitation (Summary)

An undercut crack starts at the right hand end of the wall.

1. 30ft (9m), (5b). Gain the crack with some strenuous and gymnastic moves, directly or stepping in from the left (both ways are equally awkward). Follow the crack directly to the top.

Flake Crack and Tacitation (Description)

Whatever the season, Kyloe Crag always seems a pleasant place to climb. The buttesses are more-or-less independent and because of this, and its sheltered sunny nature amongst the bracken and trees, a picnic atmosphere pervades. Should the odd shower find its way to the crag there are ample ground level roofs and overhangs under which to shelter.

On the last occasion I visited the crag, the bracken was still high, though perhaps past its luxuriant best, but the popularity of the rocks had ensured that an ample path had been trodden beneath. On stepping back from the rocks to suitably frame my subject I crossed some scree under the bracken. From one of the many voids four beady eyes anxiously looked into mine. Small, bluntly triangular heads and shiny bodies revealed the identity of two intertwined slow worms. Not snakes, much pleasanter somehow. I hadn't seen this species of small reptile since my youth. A comforting reminder that, with a little care and responsibility climbers and wildlife can co-exist even within a relatively busy environment.

The author nearly half way up Flake Crack.

The author half way up Flake Crack.

The start of Tacitation is remarkably problematical.

The two routes chosen here are of solid character within their respective grades. Flake Crack, a delectable route offering fine climbing and excellent position, is certainly no pushover for the grade. The crack extends for most of the length of the wall and fortunately the holds are positive, even if sometimes they are of a size to accept only one finger, for the wall is unrelentingly steep. Occasionally, too, it will be felt beneficial to use the wall either left or right of the crack as circumstances dictate. The final section when the crack fades is deliciously juggy. A just reward for earlier rigours.

It is often worth waiting to see just how others start Tacitation. Even so, it is frequently something of a shock, whichever way you tackle it. Afterwards the climbing is always interesting, mostly inescapably vertical, but the technical difficulty and strenuosity are nowhere near so high as in those first few undercut feet.

The crack gobbles up runners in places, but care should be taken to ensure that an runners placed can be removed withou damaging the rock. The sandstone, wit sharp flakes and pockets that are immacu late to climb upon, is of course rather sof But there is nothing soft about this rou and despite the easing of difficulty after th first few brutal feet, it provides stimulatir climbing until hands grasp the very top.

NORTHUMBERLAND—RAVENSHEUGH CRAG

RAVENSHEUGH CRAG: The Trouser Legs, The Crescent.

Map Ref: NY 012988.

Guidebooks: *Rock Climbing in Northern England* by Birkett & White. *Northumberland* by Northumberland Mountaineering Club.

Attitude: Generally faces north west but the climbs described are situated on the west faces of the pinnacles.

Altitude: 1, 300ft (400m).

Rock: Sandstone.

Access: This crag lies further along the plateau that runs below Simonside North Face and the best approach is initially as for Simonside. The hamlet of Great Tosson, near Rothbury, lies below the hills of Simonside. Drive through Great Tosson, following the picnic area signs up the hill. This is the road to Lordenshaw, and after a couple of miles, the Forestry Commission car park/picnic area appears on the right. From the left end of the car park (opposite end to the track with the locked gate), take a path through the forest. This picks up a red-marked trail following a break leading up through the forest. After a little way, a burn appears on the left and soon after this a forestry road is reached. Follow this out of the woods and continue to contour around the hillside until the rocks of Simonside North Face are seen on the summit of the high plateau to the left. Keep along the track bearing right to follow the edge of the plateau right of the plantation. This leads to a stile over a fence from where a path leads in a short distance directly to the top of the crag. An easy, broad grassy gully leads down and the large distinct pinnacles are immediately visible to your left as you descend (1 hour).

Observations: The two large pinnacles provide superbly steep and gymnastic climbing. The rock is first class, sandstone at its very best, and the climbing is both strenuous and technically exacting. The routes selected do get the afternoon sunshine and are often in condition although the crag's position, perched on the edge of this exposed hillside, is open to any prevailing Westerlies.

The climber on The Crescent is at the point where one enters the rift.

RAVENSHEUGH CRAG: The Trouser Legs, The Crescent

THE TROUSER LEGS: 50ft (15m), E1 (5b).
First Ascent: Hugh Banner (*circa* 1970).
THE CRESCENT: 45ft (14m), Severe.
First Ascent: Unknown.
Location: First and Second Pinnacles, Ravensheugh Crag, Simonside Hills, Northumberland.

The Trouser Legs (Summary)

The climb takes the unmistakeable feature up the west face of the First Pinnacle. Start in a little corner to the left of the 'legs'.

1. 50ft (15m), (5b). Move up to make an awkward traverse right to the bottom of the legs. Continue directly with much interest to the overhang. Rest possible. Traverse along right to a crack, pull up this to find another crack which leads to the top. Large boulders separate the First Pinnacle from the hillside and crossing them presents no problems.

The Crescent (Summary)

This great curving crack lies on the west face of the Second Pinnacle.

1. 45ft (14m). The initial crack leads to a ledge before the crack curves right and the meat of the climb begins. Hand traverse right until it feels better to climb into the slot. Move on through and continue up the far side to the top. The easiest way down follows the obvious wide crack up which you have just finished—Layback, Very Difficult.

The Trouser Legs and The Crescent (Description)

My first sighting of the unique Ravensheugh Crag was at a slide show illustrating the climbs of Northumberland. The overhanging cracks and steep faces of the First and Second Pinnacles immediately fired my enthusiasm and these first good impressions were more than fulfilled when I finally placed hand on rock.

Ravensheugh is, in general, a hard and gymnastic playground with success requiring a proficient technique and a fair degree of strength. The other dilemma is the decision whether or not to pack the rope or simply take friction boots and chalk bag. Certainly the climbs are high enough to make you want protection but often it is the starts that are the most difficult, after which little protection may be available in any case.

The Trouser Legs is one of those routes which is virtually impossible to grade. Hugh Banner, the sandstone expert who first climbed the route is noted for his soloing exploits and here he must have used to the full, the special qualities that this demands.

The Trouser Legs and The Crescent. The front of the first pinnacle can just be seen beyond the second which dominates the foreground.

climber on The Crescent near the rift.

Moving right to gain the bottom of The Trouser Legs – note the parallel flutings in the sandstone.

they hang there, the legs, most provocative- and reaching them is all of the technical ade I have assigned them here, so is the at of climbing them. Indeed there are me who would argue that 5c would be uch nearer the mark. So how do you grade is technically difficult climbing with no otection? Originally graded Hard Very Severe this route could equally be graded E3 in another area. Yet another dilemma.

Feeling good, climbing confidently, The Trouser Legs will feel ultimately satisfying, a dream sequence of movement on the very best quality sandstone.

The searing curving crack line of The Crescent up the Second Pinnacle is tech- nically much easier. However it offers highly original climbing making the climb different to most any other you will encounter. Finally tasting the intricacies of Raven- sheugh was, for me, ample reward for the wait. If you enjoy technical rock climbing, fresh air, a fine view, a dilemma or two, I'm sure you will feel the same way.

NORTHUMBERLAND—SANDY CRAG

SANDY CRAG: Sandy Crack, Angel Fingers.
Map Ref: NY 968972.
Guidebooks: *Rock Climbing in Northern England* by Birkett & White. *Northumberland* by Northumberland Mountaineering Club.
Attitude: Faces north west.
Altitude: 850ft (260m).
Rock: Sandstone.
Access: The crag lies on the hillside above the B6341 Rothbury to Otterburn road. When approaching from Rothbury the road turns through a right angle to cross Grasslees Burn (a private roads leads straight on to Midgy House—do not take this); shortly after this a gate on the left is signed Midgy House. The verge is narrow and care must be taken with parking. Follow the track through the gate until, adjacent to the house entrance, a gate leads to a small wooden footbridge leading across Darden Burn. A path then leads on and out of the ravine-like burn up the shoulder above. At the top of the shoulder the distinct rocks of Sandy Crag can be seen (30 minutes). Do not mistake some lesser rocks on the left—the large looking Sandy Crag is of a quarried appearance. On occasions the gamekeeper, based at Midgy House, requests that the grouse should not be disturbed. An alternative approach, although ultimately crossing the same area of moor, is from Grasslees further along the road. If Midgy House is passed then the distinct crags can be plainly seen, high on the moor, before Grasslees is reached.
Observations: The Sandy Crags marked on the O. S. L81 map are in fact not the crag but merely a pile of lesser boulders some distance behind. The crag itself is quite striking and the clean angular walls and buttresses give it a quarried appearance. Because of the altitude and aspect there can be quite a lot of lichen on the holds but the positive nature of the lines more than makes up for this. The crag, placed on a shoulder of the hill and partially in a little hollow, often remains quite sheltered even when a keen wind blows.

Wilf Williamson moving up the overhanging start of Sandy Crack.

SANDY CRAG: Sandy Crack, Angel Fingers

ANDY CRACK: 80ft (24m), E2 (5c).
irst Ascent: John Earl, Bob Hutchinson
irca 1975).
NGEL FINGERS: 65ft (20m), E1 (5a).
irst ascent: John Earl, Bob Hutchinson, Ian
ranston (*circa* 1975).
ocation: Sandy Crag, Northumberland.

andy Crack (Summary)

he distinct crack up the buttress on the
ght hand side of the crag is unmistakeable.
1. 80ft (24m), (5c). Climb the overhang-
g recess and go through the roof to gain
e base of the wall split by the crack. Then
imb the narrowing crack to gain a horizon-
l break some way below the top. A rest can
taken here before the wall above is
imbed directly to a slightly sandy finish.

ngel Fingers (Summary)

he distinct crack line up the buttress just
ght of a heather-filled chimney that
ounds the left end of this right-hand
ection of the crag.
1. 65ft (20m), (5a). From the left step into
e thin crack as soon as possible. Continue
eeply up the crack with some very interest-
g moves to gain the pod where the crack
idens. Continue to the horizontal break
en use the two, thin, disjointed vertical
racks to climb the wall to the top.

andy Crack and Angel Fingers
Description)

n the right end of Sandy Crag stands a
erfectly smooth pedestal of rock split by a
arrowing hand-wide crack. Elevated from
e ground the crack can be gained only by
imbing the overhanging barrier and its
tting-out roof. Another crack in a county
f sandstone cracks. Yes, but Sandy Crack is
HE crack. Irresistible, inspirational, a line
f striking genius.

Providing you meet with no obstacles in
he form of belligerent gamekeepers, the
roll over the purple-heathered moors to
andy Crag is well worthwhile. The walk is
ighly enjoyable in itself and the crag
nvironment superb. Ignore the curiously
rontosaurus shaped rocks up to the left,
nd the alarming demonic 'getback, get-

Wilf Williamson begins the awkward sequence on Angel Fingers to gain the pod.

back' staccato cry of the grouse as they whir
from hiding beneath your boots, for the
destination lies straight ahead.

The clean-walled and sharply-angled buttresses that make up the crag resemble the
features of a quarried face. Perhaps it was

once a source of building stone, for the
bottom of the crag lies in a little hollow,
suggesting material may have been removed. Hidden, too, amongst the surrounding bracken is a vast jumble of rock,
precariously perched boulders, and a num-

ber of holes to fall into. Also, what apppears to be an obvious trackway, which is most probably a natural fault, slopes its way down to the Darden Burn.

Despite the name, or any possible quarried origin, the two routes described are not sandy, apart from the top few feet as you make an exit. Even so, the first ascent of Sandy Crack must have been a remarkably bold effort for the parallel-sided crack would not have offered much security in the pre-Friend era. Today, it can be incredibly well protected, but it still has to be climbed and it is solid from start to finish. Shake the sand off the boots, preferably standing on a clean towel, before you start. The opportunity to clean them doesn't arise again.

A neck-craning start is probably as hard as anything above. But when it's over and you gain a standing position between overhanging and steep, below the crack, take the opportunity to shake out arms and mentally prepare for what lies above.

The face is shaped like an hour glass. Equally as smooth, it is devoid of positive holds apart from the crack itself. Mercifully this also means that the initial section is not vertical. The jams are good here and so, drawn by these weaknesses in Sandy Crack's defences, you summon enough psyche to start. In a few feet, the tender trap sprung, the wall rears vertical and the crack begins to taper: hand jam to finger jam to finger tip holds where you can find them.

Invigorating climbing, strength sapping yet beguiling, from crack thuggery to precarious technicality as you fight to gain the horizontal break. A welcome rest before an elegant piece of wall climbing takes you on to the finish. Then, scoop the sand to hollow a finger pocket, grasp the heather, pull over and feel the windblast sweeping across the open moor.

In most instances Angel Fingers would be classed as the climb of the crag. Here, next to something extraordinarily special it must take second place. Yet that is no reason for such an excellent climb to be forgotten. Accomplished finger jamming technique is a pre-requisite for success here, though it is very difficult to accredit a precise overall grade. Although there are some very demanding moves to be made in the crack, runners are good and the broken ground to the immediate left counters the technical difficulties. As the route fills out, the nature of the climbing changes but the finale up the whistle-clean walls remains, to the very last move, outstanding.

Sandy Crack and Angel Fingers on Sandy Crag.

NORTHUMBERLAND—SIMONSIDE NORTH FACE

SIMONSIDE NORTH FACE: Flake Chimney, Long Layback Crack.
Map Ref: NZ 025988.
Guidebooks: *Rock Climbing in Northern England* by Birkett & White. *Northumberland* by Northumberland Mountaineering Club.
Attitude: Faces north.
Altitude: 1, 300ft (400m).
Rock: Sandstone.
Access: The hamlet of Great Tosson, near Rothbury, lies below the hills of Simonside. The best way to reach the crag is to drive through Great Tosson, following the picnic area signs up the hill. This is the road to Lordenshaw and after a couple of miles the Forestry Commission car park/picnic area appears on the right. From the left end of the car park (opposite end to the track with the locked gate) take a path through the forest. This joins a red marked trail following a break leading directly up through the forest. After a little way a burn appears on the left and soon after this a forestry road is reached (this road actually emanates from the right side of the picnic area). Follow this out of the woods and continue to contour around the hillside until the rocks are seen on the summit of the higher plateau to the left. There is a large distinct boulder—the picnic boulder—beneath the rocks and a short path leads directly to it (40 minutes).

Observations: This crag forms the north face of the summit of Simonside. It occupies a tremendous position with an excellent vista looking out across the rolling Northumberland countryside to the distant Cheviot hills. Its elevation and remoteness give it a real mountain feel and this is one of its chief attractions. There are numerous climbs of interest and with an average length of around 40ft (12m) there is considerable variety. But it can be cold, and a pair of gloves and an extra top should complement the flask of hot coffee.

Looking from the summit of Simonside towards distant Cheviot.

SIMONSIDE NORTH FACE: Flake Chimney, Long Layback Crack

FLAKE CHIMNEY: 35ft (11m), Very Difficult.
First Ascent: Unknown.
LONG LAYBACK CRACK: 35ft (11m), Very Severe (4c).
First Ascent: Unknown.
Location: Boulder Face, Simonside North Face, Northumberland.

Flake Chimney (Summary)

This climb lies over to the left end, on the Boulder Face, of Simonside North Face.

 1. 35ft (11m). Follow the corner to the top.

Long Layback Crack (Summary)

Round the rib to the right of the Flake Chimney lies this unmistakable feature. A steep crack up the corner is flanked by smooth vertical walls.

 1. 35ft (11m), (4c). Climb the crack. The bold will layback, but the not so bold may seek an alternative technique.

Flake Chimney and Long Layback Crack (Description)

The setting: high above Coquet Dale and the rural market town of Rothbury, looking across the vast expanse of purple heathers, patchwork fields and rolling moors out to the distant crowned king of Northumberland. The Cheviot (2, 674ft), is reason enough for any climber who loves the hills to climb here. In the early days of climbing this was one of the most important crags in these parts, possibly prompting Geoffrey Winthrop Young to record:

'There is no nobler country than that of Northumberland as it rolls processionally northwards to the Border in great waves of coloured and historic moorland, cresting upon the skyline into sudden and surprising crags, which crown for us the magnificent walking with admirable rock climbs. May the growing tide of northern climbers flow onward as great-heartedly.'[1]

1. 1950 Guidebook published by the Northumbrian Mountaineering Club—*Northumberland A Rock Climbing Guide* foreword by Geoffrey Winthrop Young.

The author enjoying climbing on good holds on Flake Chimney.

O belay point

Flake
Chimney

Long
Layback
Crack

Flake Chimney and Long Layback Crack on Simonside North Face.

Fashions and tastes change, and today these north-facing crags are nowhere near so popular as the more accessible and technically harder sandstone outcrops elsewhere in the district. But for the hardy who make the effort, there are ample rewards. The climbing and the rock are excellent and one can always retire to the large picnic boulder below should the sunshine elude the crag for too long.

One of the crag's attractions is the proliferation of chimneys, grooves and cracks that offer short but worthwhile climbs around the Very Difficult standard. Steepness and technical difficulty is sustained but the brevity offers solace; in short, these are ideal training routes. Such a route is the Flake Chimney, which within its length is a sparkling and delightful climb.

The challenge of the Long Layback Crack is irresistible. A plumb vertical corner crack searing apart two clean cut walls instantly defines it as the classic of the area as is Cenotaph Corner to Dinas Cromlech or Gimmer Crack to Gimmer Crag. The brave will layback, posibly shunning any attempt to place runners in the awkwardly wide crack, but others may try a rather more restrained approach, using both sides of the crack itself to progress. No way is easy and the difficulties are continuous and unescapable. A single route, most certainly at the top of its grade, alone worth more than double the walk.

LIST OF FIRST ASCENTS

1926, **Black Slab**, Stanage Edge, A. T. Hargreaves.

1928, **Flake Crack**, Helsby, The Wayfarers' Club (probably Colin Kirkus).

1928, **Grooved Slab**, Helsby, The Wayfarers' Club.

1930s, **Idiot's Delight**, Great Wanney, A. P. Rossiter.

1940s, **Main Wall**, Crag Lough, B. Butcher, K. Gregory.

1943, **Great Western**, Almscliff, A. Dolphin.

1945, **Angel's Wall**, Caley Crags, A. Dolphin.

1945, **Roof Layback**, Caley Crags, A. Dolphin.

1945, **Roof of the World**, Caley Crags, A. Dolphin.

1949, **Left Unconquerable**, Stanage Edge, Tom Probert.

1949, **Right Unconquerable**, Stanage Edge, Joe Brown, Slim Sorrell, Wilf White.

1950s, **Tacitation**, Kyloe Crag, Nev Hannaby.

1950s, **Maloja**, Brimham Rocks, J. R. Lees.

1950s, **Flake Crack**, Kyloe Crag, Eric Clark, G. Lewis, Basil Butcher.

1951, **Peapod**, Curbar Edge, Joe Brown, Slim Sorrell.

1952 February, **Sin**, Stoney Middleton, Ron Moseley.

1952 March, **Croton Oil**, Rivelin Needle, R. D. Brown, Donald Wooler, Frank Fitzgerald, Five points of aid. Free: Pete Crew, Oliver Woolcock 1963.

1955, **Allan's Slab**, Brimham Rocks, A. Austin.

1956, **The Rasp**, Higgar Tor, Joe Brown.

1956, **The File**, Higgar Tor, Don Whillans.

1956, **George**, Tissington Spires, S. Read, R. Leeming, D. Carnell, P. Brown, S. Hunt climbed as an aid route. Two Points Aid: P. J. Nunn, J. Morgan November 1969. Free in 1970.

1956, **Face Route**, Gordale Scar, R. Moseley, J. Smith. Three Points Aid: K. Wood, A. Austin 1971. Free: P. Livesey, J. Sheard 1971.

1957, **Frensis Direct**, Brimham Rocks, A. Austin.

1957, **Bachelor's Left Hand**, Hen Cloud, Don Whillans.

1957, **Great North Road**, Millstone Edge, Joe Brown. Previously pegged by P. Biven, T. Peck.

1957, **Minion's Way**, Brimham Rocks, A. Austin/D. Gray apparently climbed the route on the same day.

1959, **Venus**, Crummackdale, B. Evans.

1959, **Pothole Wall**, Willersley Castle Crag, S. Read, B. Jackson with aid. Free: D. Hadlum, D. Gray 1960.

960 May 22, **Medusa**, Ravensdale, D. Johnson, D. Mellor.

960s, **Nightwatch**, Whitestone Cliff, T. Sullivan.

961, **Jordu**, Peak Scar, T. Sullivan, V. Tosh.

961, **Pianississimo**, Peak Scar, T. Sullivan, V. Tosh.

961, **Kirkby Wall**, Malham Cove, A. Austin, B. Evans.

963, **Darius**, High Tor, O. Woolcock, C. Rowland, P. Nunn with aid. One Point Aid: E. Drummond, T. Proctor 1971. Free: P. Livesey 1974.

963 December 22, **The Candle**, Twistleton Scars, A. Austin.

963 December 22, **Priority**, Twistleton Scars, B. Evans.

964 January 1, **Evening Star**, Twistleton Scars, A. Greenbank.

964, **John Peel**, Tissington Spires, P. Williams, J. H. Amies.

964, **Wombat**, Malham Cove, R. Barley, D. Gray.

965, **The Arches**, Back Bowden Doors, Rodney Wison.

968, **Golden Tower**, Les Ainsworth, Ian Cowell (alternate leads).

968, **Lorraine**, Bowden Doors, Malcom Rowe.

969, **Main Wall**, Bowden Doors, M. Rowe.

970s, **Merry Monk**, Lazonby, A. Beatty, J. Simpson, J. Workman.

970s, **Psycho**, Caley Crags, R. Fawcett.

970s, **The Trouser Legs**, Ravensheugh Crag, H. Banner.

971, **Fern Hill**, Cratcliffe Tor, Keith Myhill with One Point Aid. Same or similar line climbed earlier by P. Harding, V. Ridgway.

972, **Great Wall**, Great Wanney, M. Foggan, H. Banner.

974, **Angel Fingers**, Sandy Crag, John Earl, Bob Hutchinson, Ian Cranston.

975, **London Wall**, Millstone Edge, John Allen, Steve Bancroft. Previously egged by P. Biven, T. Peck.

975, **Sandy Crack**, Sandy Crag, John Earl, Bob Hutchinson.

976, **Northumberland Wall**, Bob Hutchinson, John Earl.

978, **The Tube**, Back Bowden Doors, Bob Hutchinson, John Earl.

978, **Poseidon Adventure**, Bowden Doors, S. Blake.

GRADED LIST OF ROCK CLIMBS

(alphabetical order within each grade)

E5

London Wall (6a)   Millstone Edge
Psycho (6b)   Caley Crags

E4

Poseidon Adventure (6a)   Bowden Doors
The Tube (5c)   Back Bowden Doors

E3

Face Route (5c)   Gordale Scar

E2

Darius (5c)   High Tor
Fern Hill (5c)   Cratcliffe Tor
Left Unconquerable (5c)   Stanage Edge
Northumberland Wall (5b)   Great Wanney
Sandy Crack (5c)   Sandy Crag
The Golden Tower (5c)   Anglezarke Quarry
The Rasp (5b)   Higgar Tor
Wombat (5c)   Malham Cove

E1

Angel Fingers (5a)   Sandy Crag
Frensis Direct (5b)   Brimham Rocks
George (5b)   Tissington Spires
Right Unconquerable (5b)   Stanage Edge
The Candle (5b)   Twistleton Scars
The Trouser Legs (5b)   Ravensheugh Crag
Peapod (5b)   Curbar Edge

Hard Very Severe

Bachelor's Left Hand (5a)   Hen Cloud
Croton Oil (5a)   Rivelin Needle
Great North Road (5a)   Millstone Edge
Great Wall (5b)   Great Wanney
John Peel (5a)   Tissington Spires
Kirkby Wall (5b)   Malham Cove
Main Wall (5a)   Bowden Doors
Merry Monk (5a)   Lazonby
Minion's Way (5b)   Brimham Rocks
Tacitation (5b)   Kyloe Crag
The Arches (5a)   Back Bowden Doors

Very Severe

Angel's Wall (5a)   Caley Crags
Flake Crack (5a)   Helsby
Great Western (5a)   Almscliff
Long Layback Crack (4c)   Simonside North Face
Lorraine (5a)   Bowden Doors
Medusa (4b)   Ravensdale

Pianississimo (4c)	Peak Scar
Pothole Wall (5a)	Willersley Castle Crag
Roof Layback (5a)	Caley Crags
Roof of the World (5a)	Caley Crags
Sin (4c)	Stoney Middleton
The File (4c)	Higgar Tor
Venus (4c)	Crummackdale

Mild Very Severe

Allan's Crack (4b)	Brimham Rocks
Priority (4a)	Twistleton Scars

Hard Severe

Black Slab (4a)	Stanage Edge
Evening Star	Twistleton Scars
Grooved Slab (4a)	Helsby
Idiot's Delight (4a)	Great Wanney
Maloja (4a)	Brimham Rocks
Nightwatch (4a)	Whitestone Cliff

Severe

Flake Crack (4a)	Kyloe Crag
Main Wall	Crag Lough
The Crescent	Ravensheugh Crag

Very Difficult

Flake Chimney	Simonside North Face
Jordu	Peak Scar

TICK LIST OF CLIMBS

AREA 1: LANCASHIRE

Anglezarke Quarry
- [ ] E2 (5c) The Golden Tower

Helsby
- [ ] VS (5a) Flake Crack
- [ ] HS (4a) Grooved Slab

AREA 2: THE PEAK DISTRICT

Cratcliffe Tor
- [ ] E2 (5c) Fern Hill

Curbar Edge
- [ ] E1 (5b) Peapod

Hen Cloud
- [ ] HVS (5a) Bachelor's Left Hand

Higgar Tor
- [ ] E2 (5b) The Rasp
- [ ] Vs (4c) The File

High Tor
- [ ] E2 (5c) Darius

Millstone Edge
- [ ] HVS (5a) Great North Road
- [ ] E5 (6a) London Wall

Ravensdale
- [ ] VS (4b) Medusa

Rivelin Needle
- [ ] HVS (5a) Croton Oil

Stanage Edge:
- [ ] HS (4a) Black Slab
- [ ] E2 (5c) Left Unconquerable
- [ ] E1 (5b) Right Unconquerable

Stoney Middleton
- [ ] VS (4c) Sin

Tissington Spires
- [ ] HVS (5a) John Peel
- [ ] E1 (5b) George

Willersley Castle Crag
- [ ] VS (5a) Pothole Wall

AREA 3: YORKSHIRE

Almscliff
- [ ] VS (5a) Great Western

Brimham Rocks
- [ ] HVS (5b) Minion's Way
- [ ] HS (4a) Maloja
- [ ] E1 (5b) Frensis Direct
- [ ] MVS (4b) Allan's Crack

Caley Crags
- [ ] E5 (6b) Psycho
- [ ] VS (5a) Angel's Wall
- [ ] VS (5a) Roof Layback
- [ ] VS (5a) Roof of the World

Crummackdale
- [ ] VS (4c) Venus

Gordale Scar
- [ ] E3 (5c) Face Route

Malham Cove
- [ ] HVS (5b) Kirkby Wall
- [ ] E2 (5c) Wombat

Twistleton Scars
- [ ] E1 (5b) The Candle
- [ ] HS Evening Star
- [ ] MVS (4a) Priority

AREA 4: NORTH YORK MOORS

Peak Scar
- [ ] VD Jordu
- [ ] VS (4c) Pianississimo

Whitestone Cliff
- [ ] HS (4a) Nightwatch

AREA 5: CUMBRIA

Lazonby
- [ ] HVS (5a) Merry Monk

AREA 6: NORTHUMBERLAND

Back Bowden Doors
- [ ] E4 (5c) The Tube
- [ ] HVS (5a) The Arches

Bowden Doors
- [ ] HVS (5a) Main Wall
- [ ] VS (5a) Lorraine
- [ ] E4 (6a) Poseidon Adventure

Crag Lough
- [ ] S Main Wall

Great Wanney
- [ ] HS (4a) Idiot's Delight
- [ ] HVS (5b) Great Wall
- [ ] E2 (5b) Northumberland Wall

Kyloe Crag
- [ ] S (4a) Flake Crack
- [ ] HVS (5b) Tacitation

Ravensheugh Crag
- [ ] E1 (5b) The Trouser Legs
- [ ] S The Crescent

Sandy Crag
- [ ] E2 (5c) Sandy Crack
- [ ] E1 (5a) Angel Fingers

Simonside North Face
- [ ] VD Flake Chimney
- [ ] VS (4c) Long Layback Crack